The tower, Llanddewi Breifi, Cardiganshire

THE OLD PARISH CHURCHES
OF SOUTH-WEST WALES

Mike Salter

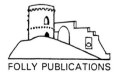

FOLLY PUBLICATIONS

ACKNOWLEDGEMENTS

The illustrations in this book are the product of the author's fieldwork in Wales between 1978 and 1994. The author measured and drew plans of the churches on site, took all the photographs, and also drew the sketches and maps. The old postcards on pages 54, 68, 77 and inside the front cover are reproduced from originals in his collection. Thanks are due to Max Barfield who provided word processor facilities, checked the text, and made available a camera with which many of the photographs were taken.

ABOUT THIS BOOK

This book completes a set of four volumes describing the architecture, funerary monuments and furnishings up to c1760 to be seen in about 800 ancient parochial churches in Wales. The index of churches at the back includes not only those appearing in this book but also the other three volumes which do not feature indexes.

All the plans are reproduced to a scale of 1:400. The buildings were measured in metres and metric scales only are given. Hatching is used to show periods of work as indicated on the master key on page 7. Space did not allow a key beside every plan.

Luckily the boundary and name changes of British counties in 1974 has not really affected the area covered by this book. The spelling of place names is much more of a problem. Throughout Wales there is considerable variation between the spellings given in the Royal Commission on Ancient and Historical Monuments (R.C.A.H.M) inventories, in the various Ordnance Survey Map editions which have appeared since World War Two, on the name boards which some of the churches have, on road signs, on village name signs, in diocesan records and in various guide books and other publications. The intention has been to use whatever spelling appears to be most commonly now in use. Dedications, where there are also some variations, have been similarly treated.

With the sole exception of the Forest of Dean volume all the churches books in the series of which this is the twentieth volume (see list on inside of back cover) exclude Late Georgian and Victorian art and architecture except for noting additions and repairs to older buildings. This is not say that buildings later than the 1760s are necessarily less attractive, less interesting, or less worthy of study. It is just that the author has decided to concentrate on pre-Reformation and early post-Reformation buildings. Besides, in counties with considerable industrial conurbations such as Staffordshire, describing later churches as well could double the amount of material to be included. All the books include Ordnance Survey Grid references (these are the letters and digits after the place names) and are intended as field guides easily carried in a knapsack or shoulder bag.

This book is intentionally very much a catalogue of dates and names, etc, and is intended as a work of reference rather than to be read from cover to cover. Little is said about the setting or atmosphere of churches. This would require more space and has already been done by other writers for some of the most visited buildings. Some churches do not require much comment on the basis of the parameters set as above, yet they may be very interesting because of features outside the scope of this book, or particularly attractively located. Visit as many as you can and judge for yourself.

ABOUT THE AUTHOR

Mike Salter is 40 and has been a professional writer and publisher since he went on the Government Enterprise Allowance Scheme in 1988. He is particularly interested in the planning and layout of medieval buildings and has a huge collection of plans of churches and castles he has measured during tours (mostly by bicycle and motorcycle) of England, Ireland, Scotland and Wales since 1968. Wolverhampton born and bred, Mike now lives in an old cottage beside the Malvern Hills. His other interests include walking, model railways, morris dancing, folk music and playing percussion instruments.

Laugharne Church

CONTENTS

Maps and lists of rebuilt churches appear at the end of the gazetteers

INTRODUCTION

Christianity was flourishing in Wales by the 6th century, the era in which St David established the community which came in time to bear his name. The large number of churches with circular raised enclosures and/or names beginning with Llan, meaning a religious site, indicate that many chapels and churches existed in South-West Wales before 1115 when Bernard, a protege of Henry I, was appointed bishop of St Davids and re-organisation of the local churches on Norman rather than Celtic lines began. Nothing of note survives of any early buildings but chapels like that of St Non and a vestry at Rhoscrowther are said to lie on their sites. Except for the church of St Davids itself they would have only been tiny single chambers of wood or unmortared stone with thatched roofs, few (if any) windows, and one plain narrow doorway. The only relics now surviving earlier than the 12th century are crosses like that at Carew and tomb stones inscribed with crosses or inscriptions in early forms of writing like Ogham.

The present parochial system was gradually organised during the 12th century. Sometimes bishops would insist on the provision of churches in certain places but often the initiative came from the lay lord of the manor who would have a church built close to his castle. Some 12th and 13th century churches were single chambers but others had two compartments, a nave in which the congregation would stand (the infirm would sit on the floor or on a bench against a wall) and a chancel just big enough to contain the altar and attendant priest. There would be a doorway in the nave south wall and sometimes another opposite in the north wall. After the fashion for the clergy to lead the congregation in a procession around the church and churchyard on certain holy days passed secondary doorways were less useful and many have been blocked up. In the 12th century doorways usually had round arches, and there would be a few windows with tiny round arched outer openings and widely splayed embrasures towards the interior. Roofs would be of thatch or stone slabs laid on a closely spaced series of simple trusses. Floors would be covered with rushes. Apart from a bench as noted above the only fittings would be a font for baptisms and an altar consisting of a stone slab supported at each end by other slabs set on end.

Simple nave and chancel church at Pontfaen

Window, Llanfair Ar Y Bryn   *St Bride's Church, Pembrokeshire*

In South-West Wales church remains which can be safely dated prior to the year 1200 are few. Walling with small round headed windows survives at Penbryn and Llanfair Ar Y Bryn. Several churches, such as Gumfreston and Hayscastle, have Norman style round arches between the nave and chancel and may be late 12th century. In England the round arch was out of favour by c1210 but masons in South-West Wales retained that form well into the 13th century. However there is a single arch of c1175 at St David's Cathedral and the thick nave and chancel walling of a former monastic church at St Clears may be still earlier, whilst the tower at Manorbier may be of c1200. Square fonts with scallops underneath are very common. They are called Norman in the gazetteers as some may be as early as the 1170s although the style may have remained in vogue in South Wales until the 1230s.

The 13th century saw a boom in the construction and rebuilding of churches in Wales. Two thirds of the churches in this book have structural remains likely to be of that period, although again close dating is difficult because documentary evidence is mostly lacking, the plain nature of nearly all the work, and the amount of restoration. At Llanbadarn Fawr is a large but plain cruciform church with a central tower raised on four pointed arches and transepts. Lighting is by pointed headed slit windows now called lancets. Two other Cardiganshire churches, Llanddewi Breifi and Llanfihangel Creuddyn were also built on this plan. Transepts, built either singly or as a matching pair, are common, especially in the southern half of Pembrokeshire and the coastal fringe of Carmarthenshire which were areas ruled by Normans, but the only other instance of a central tower is at Laugharne, which is 14th century, and more English in design than its neighbours. So that masses at altars in transepts could be synchronised with those being said at the main altar in the chancel a hagioscope or squint was often provided. In some churches the squint is no mere shaft through the wall as in England but a passage big enough to walk through having its own window.

Aisles flanking the nave and providing extra space for an increased congregation are uncommon in South-West Wales. Just five churches, Carew Cheriton, Tenby, Llandysul, Manorbier, and Steynton, have aisles on both sides. Carew has a tower like those of SW England and in its plan (see page 7) and elevations is quite unlike those of neighbouring churches, the result of the local lords being Devon-based. Tenby is a huge church which served a prosperous borough. The other three churches have arcades of plain pointed arches cut through older walls, parts of which remain in the square piers. About twenty churches have a single aisle. Commonly this is as wide and lofty as the nave and has given rise to the expression double-naved churches. Sometimes there is doubt as to which was the original nave. Most of these buildings are in Carmarthenshire. The town churches of Carmarthen and Haverfordwest St Mary had aisles by 1300 and that of St Mary at Pembroke is not much later. Elsewhere the addition seems to have often only been made in the late 15th or early 16th century.

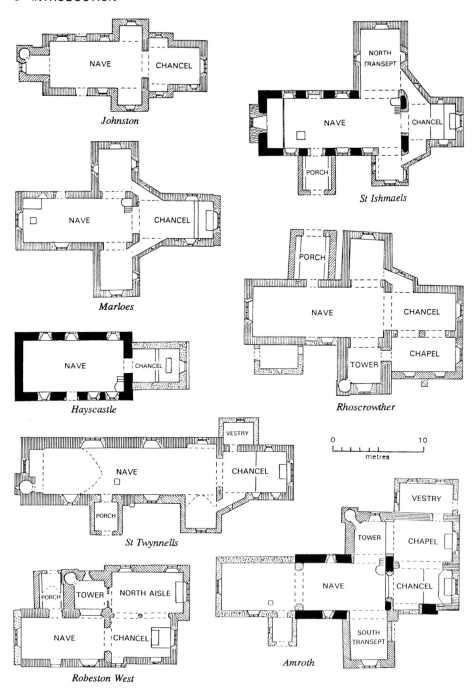

Johnston

St Ishmaels

Marloes

Hayscastle

Rhoscrowther

St Twynnells

Robeston West

Amroth

PLANS OF PEMBROKESHIRE CHURCHES

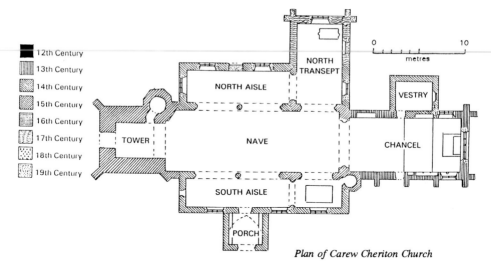

12th Century
13th Century
14th Century
15th Century
16th Century
17th Century
18th Century
19th Century

0   10
metres

NORTH TRANSEPT

NORTH AISLE

VESTRY

TOWER

NAVE

CHANCEL

SOUTH AISLE

PORCH

Plan of Carew Cheriton Church

At Manorbier both nave and aisles are stone-vaulted, and several other churches in the Norman ruled areas have vaulted naves, whilst vaults over smaller spaces such as transepts, chapels, porches, and the lowest stages of towers are very common. The vaults are usually plain pointed tunnels, but crude rib-vaults occur occasionally as at Gumfreston. These vaults in conjunction with squints and lofty, slender towers sometimes set transeptal positions really set the churches of the Normanised southern half of Pembrokeshire apart from not only their Welsh neighbours but from English and Irish churches as well. The tower of St Mary's at Haverfordwest, a fine church more typically English than most in Wales, has a late medieval fan vault.

Vaulted interior, St Twynnells

Tower at Steynton

Tower at St Florence

In the parts of South-West Wales ruled by the Normans an original simple bellcote usually perched on the west gable would often eventually be superseded by a tower. Most of these towers appear loftier than many of the counterparts in England, although this is partly because some of them, such as Hodgeston, are quite slender. In undulating terrain towers needed to be lofty to be effective as belfries and landmarks. It has been claimed that the towers were also look-out points and refuges in times of unrest although many of them may post-date the defeat of the Welsh princes in the 1280s and the pacification of the area. Where dateable features survive they tend to be late 15th century, but it seems that many of the towers are of c1270-1340 and were simply remodelled towards the end of the medieval period. Certainly a few new towers were then built, like Caeo, a rare instance of a tower in the poorer upland areas left under Welsh control. Some towers, like Ciffig, have a fireplace on an upper storey and were habitable by a priest either temporarily or permanently but it does not appear that any of them were actually indended to be defensible. Llawhaden has an interesting instance of a 13th century tower and its stair turret incorporated into a larger 14th century tower. This tower lies in a transeptal position, a layout also found in several other churches such as Gumfreston, St Florence, and Monkton. At Stackpole Elidor the tower lies beyond a north transept whilst Manorbier has a tower of c1200 tucked into the angle between the chancel and north transept. The splendid and typically late medieval English tower at Carew Cheriton has already been noted.

| *Tower at Jeffreyston* | *Tower at Reynalton* | *Tower at St Daniels* |

The principal relics of the 14th century are churches at Laugharne and Llawhaden, already mentioned, and a cruciform church, originally monastic, at Kidwelly. The latter has a contemporary vestry beside the chancel and a south porch, and in c1400 a tower and broach spire were added on the north side of the nave, where the tower base could act as a second porch. Much of Llanstephen and Lamphrey churches are also 14th century. By this time complex window tracery with floral and geometrical forms had evolved through intermediate stages of putting lancets together in twos and threes and then piercing the spandrels between their heads with circles and quatrefoils. However unrestored windows in the resulting Geometrical and Decorated styles are uncommon in Wales. The sedilia or priests' seats at Hodgeston with their richly cusped and crocketed heads utilising the newly adopted ogival arch give an idea of how rich the Decorated style could be on occasion. Many of the transepts seem to have been added in this period but none call for individual comment.

In some areas small simple churches consisting of a single chamber or a nave and chancel often of uncertain date have remained adequate throughout the centuries. If not too heavily restored these churches, such as Mynt and Penbryn on the Cardiganshire coast, can have considerable charm and interest. Penbryn has a west porch, a feature also found in churches like Gumfreston where the tower is not at the west end. Churchyard crosses thought to have been used for occasional outdoor preaching are found on the south side of several churches, notably that of Jeffreyston.

The late 15th and early 16th century was a boom period for work on Welsh churches although the effect in South-West Wales was uneven. In Pembrokeshire substantial parts of the churches of Nevern, Newport, Slebech, and Tenby are of this period, and there is a detached chantry chapel at Angle, but otherwise work was confined to minor repairs and rebuilding and the insertion of a window here and there. In Carmarthenshire more work was carried out, aisles and chantry chapels to contain altars for masses of the souls of the departed being built, and towers added or rebuilt. Those churches not too heavily restored nearly all have windows and doorways of this period. The flatter four-centred arch was now in vogue for doorways and windows, although windows with square heads are common too. Tracery is generally minimal, the lights simply rising to arched and cusped tops. Gradually as the 16th century worn on the cusping disappears and the tops of the lights become rounded.

Porch entrance at Monkton

Former south doorway at Wiston

Tower doorway at Slebech

West doorway at Tenby

Font, St Issells   *Font, Hodgeston*

Font, Lamphey   *Font, Camrose*

Font, Cenarth

Effigy at Llangwm   *Bench End, Haverfordwest*

By the time of the Reformation in the 1530s churches that had been bare and poorly lighted in the 12th and 13th centuries had been transformed. Large new windows admitted more light although they were sometimes filled with stained glass depicting Biblical scenes, the lives of saints, or heraldry of benefactors. Fragments of the latter category remain at Laugharne. In many churches paving slabs and the nave and floor tiles around the altar had been introduced, although some had earth floors covered with rushes until the 18th and 19th centuries. Benches were provided for the congregation. Sermons were now fashionable and pulpits began to be installed. The chancel was often divided off by a screen. Sometimes a loft was provided above it for use by actors and musicians, organs then being very rare, and plays being of importance to convey God's Word to congregations before services were held in English or Welsh rather than Latin. Such lofts were known as rood-lofts from the Rood or crucifix attached to them. No original examples survive in South-West Wales (although one was been reconstructed at Llandeloy) but stairs built into the nave SE or SW corner often indicate their former existence. In some small and poor churches the rood was attached to a beam for which corbels can sometimes be seen.

Much woodwork and stonework inside was painted or gilded to produce a riot of colour. Traces of murals can be seen at Eglwyscymyn. Others must survive hidden elsewhere under coats of whitewash applied in later periods. It should be remembered that many murals, carvings, memorials, and stained glass windows thought to be too popish were removed, altered, or concealed after the Reformation. Wooden chests originally used to store plate often survive, and there are plenty of ancient fonts, which have proved more likely to survive drastic rebuilding and restoration than anything else. Many date from c1200 as already noted. Pencarrog has an interesting example with four heads; another from Llantyssiligogo has been removed to Cenarth. Of later fonts there is a rare five sided example at Bletherston, and Pendine has a seven sided example, but the majority have round or octagonal bowls.

Effigy at Stackpole Elidor

The large number of empty tomb recesses in the churches show that many medieval effigies have been lost. About twenty survive, mostly in Pembrokeshire and all in the Norman-ruled areas. The earliest are the late 13th century lady at Kidwelly and the knights at Lawrenny and Nolton. A very fine tomb and canopy remain at Stackpole Elidor where there are several other effigies, and there are other collections at Carew Cheriton and Tenby. A common form of medieval memorial, especially in the

Tomb at Stackpole Elidor

Welsh dominated areas, was a slab on which a cross was incised or left raised. Sometimes the crosses are floriated and they can be quite ornate. At Monkton are indents cut in a slab of lost brasses of a family group of two kneeling adults and children. The only surviving brass showing a figure is a crude engraving of the Commonwealth period at St Mary's at Haverfordwest, but there is an inscription at Robeston West. Effigies of the post-Reformation period are few although there are good examples at Stackpole, Carew Cheriton, and Monkton. Memorials of this period are mostly fairly simple tablets although sometimes embellished with symbols of death, heraldry, architectural surrounds, or emblems referring to a trade or claim to fame.

Tomb of Rogert Lort and family at Stackpole Elidor Church

Llanelli Church, mostly rebuilt in the 19th century.

Little work was carried out on the fabric of Welsh parish churches during the period 1550 to 1800 beyond minor maintenance, the insertion of a window here and there, and the occasional adding or rebuilding of a tower or porch. Apart from the south transept at Slebech and the rebuilding of the large nave and tower at Cardigan c1702-6 what work there is in South-West Wales of this period tends to be modest and rather rustic like the chapel arcade at Minwear.

By the early 19th century many of the churches were in a poor state of repair and those now in use at Llandeloy and Pontfaen actually lay in ruins. Between then and First World War almost all of them were restored, in many cases the work amounting to complete, or almost complete, rebuilding. Many old furnishings and monuments which had survived the Reformation or had accumulated since were swept away as floors were relaid, heating systems installed, new roofs provided, vestries and porches added, and the majority of windows repaired or replaced. Some, usually where nothing but a single farm lies anywhere near, like LLanfihangel Penbedw and Castell Dwyfan, have now become derelict again and others like St Daniels are decayed and little used.

FURTHER READING

Archeologia Cambrensis (published annually).
A Guide to Welsh Churches, R.W. Soden, 1984
Companion Guide to South Wales, Peter Howel & Elizabeth Beazley, Collins, 1977.
Every Single One, Visiting the Churches of Pembrokeshire, Peter Ball, 1986.
Lost Churches of Wales and The Marches, Paul R. Davies & Susan Lloyd-Fern, 1990.
Pamphlets etc for Gumfreston, Kidwelly, Llandyssul, Penbryn, St Ishmael, Walton W.
Royal Commission on Ancient and Historical Monuments (R.C.A.H.M.) inventories for
    Carmarthen (1917) and Pembroke (1925), H.M.S.O.

A GLOSSARY OF TERMS

Ashlar — Masonry of blocks with even faces and square edges.
Aumbry — A recess for storing books or vessels.
Batter — A slope on a wall face.
Cable Moulding — Norman moulding imitating a twisted cord.
Cartouche — Ornately framed tablet, usually elliptical, with arms and inscription.
Chancel — The eastern part of a church used by the clergy and choir.
Chancel Arch — The arch between a chancel and a nave.
Chevrons — Ornament with a series of Vs forming a zig-zag.
Corbel Table — A series of corbels or brackets carrying a wall-plate or parapet.
Crenellation — Indents (crenels) in the top of a parapet.
Cruciform Church — Cross-shaped church with transepts forming the arms of the cross.
Dog Tooth — A four-cornered stair placed diagonally and raised pyramidally.
Easter Sepulchre — A recess in a chancel given an effigy of Christ at Easter.
Elizabethan — Of the time of Elizabeth I (reigned 1558-1603).
Fan Vault — A vault with fan-like tracery emanating from the corners and middle.
Fleuron — Decorative carved shape like a flower or leaf.
Four-Centred-Arch — Low flat arch with each curve drawn from two compass points.
Impost — A wall bracket, often moulded, to support the end of an arch.
Hoodmould — A projecting moulding above an arch or lintel to throw off water.
Jacobean — Of the time of James I (King of England and Wales 1603 to 1625).
Jamb — The side of a doorway, window, or other opening.
Lancet — A long narrow single-light window, usually with a pointed head.
Light — A compartment of a window.
Lintel — A horizontal stone or beam spanning an opening.
Mullion — A vertical member dividing the lights of a window.
Nave — The part of a church in which the congregation sits or stands.
Norman — Architectural style current in Wales during the 12th century.
Ogham — An ancient form of script with lines across an edge.
Ogival Arch — Arch of oriental origin with both convex and concave curves.
Parapet — A wall for protection at any sudden drop.
Piscina — Basin with a drain through the wall. Used for washing mass vessels.
Plinth — The projecting base of a wall.
Quoins — Dressed (smooth faced) stones at the corners of a building.
Rere-arch — An arch over the inner side of a doorway or window embrasure.
Respond — A half-pier bonded into a wall to carry one end of an arch.
Rood Loft — A loft between nave and chancel with a crucifix mounted upon it.
Saddleback — A plain gabled roof (i.e. without a parapet) upon a tower.
Scalloped — A surface treated with a series of truncated half-cones.
Sedilia — Seats (usually three) for priests in the south wall of a chancel.
Spandrel — The surface between two arches.
Squint — A hole or passage allowing a view of the high altar from a side altar.
Tracery — Intersecting ribwork in the upper part of a later Gothic window.
Transom — A horizontal member dividing the lights of a window.
Victorian — Of the time of Queen Victoria (reigned 1837-1901.)
Voussoir — Small wedge shaped stone used as part of an arch.
Wagon Roof — A roof with closely set rafters with arch braces. Such a roof may be left uncovered or may be panelled or plastered (ceiled).

GAZETTEER OF CARDIGANSHIRE CHURCHES

BETTWS BLEDRWS
Dedication Unknown SN 596520

Except for part of the west wall the church was rebuilt in 1886.

BRONGWYN
Dedication Unknown SN 287437

The form of the west doorway suggests that the small single chamber may be 12th century. One north window could be that early, or later medieval.

CARDIGAN
St Mary SN 181461

The large nave has several two and three light windows with round arched lights under square heads. They belong to the rebuilding of 1702-3. The large 16th century west tower collapsed soon after and was also rebuilt. The chancel is 14th century, but apart from ornate piscina its features are renewed. There are fragments of old glass in the upper part of the east window and two corbels have grinning faces. The south porch is early 17th century. The font is 15th century.

Cardigan Church

14th Century 18th Century
17th Century 19th Century

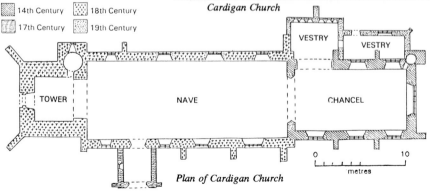

VESTRY VESTRY

TOWER NAVE CHANCEL

0   10

metres

Plan of Cardigan Church

CELLAN   *Dedication Unknown*   SN 614497

A 14th century porch has been added to a 13th century nave and chancel.

LAMPETER   *St Peter*   SN 576484

The church was rebuilt in 1869 but contains 17th century monuments.

LLANARTH   *Dedication Unknown*   SN 423578

The west tower with a NE stair turret is 15th century. The long nave and the chancel have medieval masonry but no old openings.

LLANBADARN FAWR   *St Padarn*   SN 599810

A Celtic monastery here died out about the time of the erection of the present large cruciform church in the early 13th century. There are no aisles or chapels, just a low crossing tower no less than 12m square carried on plain pointed arches with a nave, transepts, and chancel of the sort of austere design the Cistercians would have approved of. The chancel has three 15th century windows at the east end but the other windows are all original narrow lancets. There are empty tomb recesses in the transept end walls. The font is also 13th century. Only the small vestry and the large porch on the south side of the nave are of the 1870 restoration when the box-pews were removed. In the south transept are an old chest and 8th century crosses. The chancel contains monuments to the Powells of Nanteos and the Pryses of Gogerddan.

Llanbadarn Fawr Church

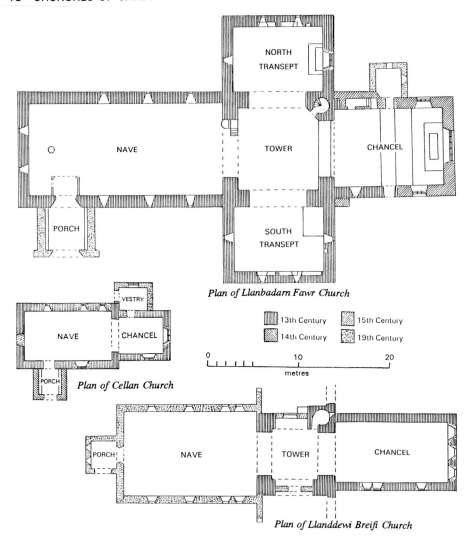

Plan of Llanbadarn Fawr Church

13th Century   15th Century
14th Century   19th Century

0   10   20
metres

Plan of Cellan Church

Plan of Llanddewi Breifi Church

LLANBADARN ODWYN   *St Padarn*   SN 634605

The chancel inclines northwards. The interior was relined with breeze-blocks in 1952.

LLANCYNFELIN   *St Cynfelin*   SN 645922

The old features comprise a 14th century font, a fragment of the former screen reused as a canopy reredos, and the blocked 13th century nave north doorway.

LLANDDEWI ABERARTH   *St David*   SN 477634

The small west tower with a pointed tunnel vault may be late 13th century. The nave and chancel have no ancient features.

Llanddewi Aberarth Church

LLANDDEWI BREIFI *St David* SN 664554

The north and south plain pointed arches under the early 13th century crossing tower have been blocked up since the transepts collapsed in the 1770s. The chancel is original but has no ancient features. The wide nave and west porch are entirely of the rebuilding of 1874. The 7th century stones in the chancel are relics of a clas or Celtic monastery here which survived until 1287.

Llanarth Church   *Llanddewi Breifi Church*

Llandysul Church

LLANDYSUL *St Tysul* SN 419407

This church is known to have had a thatched roof until 1783. It is entered through the vaulted lower stage of a massive 14th century west tower with a NE stair turret. The nave and aisles with arcades of three plain pointed arches are probably all 13th century. The south aisle has a squint into the short but wide chancel which is probably late medieval. Behind the NE respond is the stair to the former rood loft. There is an ancient altar stone in the Lady Chapel. The ancient Velver Stone bears an Ogham inscription.

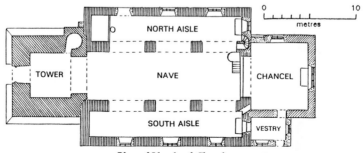

Plan of Llandysul Church

Llanssantffraid Church

LLANFAIR CLYDOGAU   *St Mary*   SN 625513

The medieval single chamber has a south wall and windows of the 1888 rebuilding.

LLANFAIR ORLLYN   *St Mary*   SN 367410

Some of the nave masonry may be medieval. The other features are 19th century.

Llanfair Orllyn Church

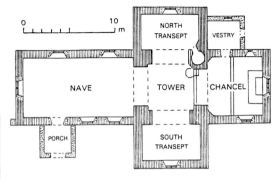

Plan of Llanfihangel Creuddyn Church

Llanfihangel Creuddyn Church

LLANFIHANGEL CREUDDYN *St Michael* SN 665761

This is a smaller mid 13th century copy of Llanbardarn Fawr church but with shallower transepts and with the lancets replaced during the restoration of 1871 by windows of two lights. There is no tracery in the belfry windows which are probably 16th century. The nave and chancel have barrel ceilings.

LLANGOEDMORE *St Cyrumo* SN 199459

The nave is perhaps 17th century. The chancel of the same length may be 18th century. All the windows are 19th century. The chancel arch is unusually deep.

LLANGYBI *St Gybi* SN 612533

The west doorway dates the small nave and chancel as 13th century. All the windows and the porch and vestry are early or late 19th century.

LLANILAR *St Hilary* SN 624751

The single main chamber with a later king-post roof and the west tower are probably 13th century. East of the present doorway are original blocked north and south doorways, and one small original lancet survives in the north wall by the altar. In the Victorian porch is a stone carved with interlace. There is a rare seven sided font.

LLANINA *St Ina* SN 405599

The small nave and chancel have old walling but no ancient features. In the nave is one old beam from the screen with a pattern of oak twigs.

LLANLLWCHAIARN *Dedication Unknown* SN 390574

In the church of 1865 are an old font and a hatchment with Royal Arms of 1621.

LLANRHYSTYD MEFONYDD *St Rhystydd* SN 538697

The tower was given buttresses and a broach spire in a rebuilding of c1850.

Llanilar Church

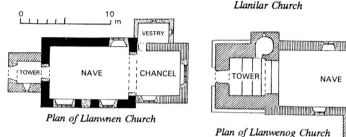

Plan of Llanwnen Church

Plan of Llanwenog Church

LLANSSANTFFRAID   *St Bridget*   SN 514675

A 15th century west tower adjoins a 19th century single chamber containing old box pews and having a slate-hung south wall. Of the chapel of St Non in Llanon parts of the north and west walls remain among brambles and rubble.

LLANTYSSILIGOGO   *St Tysull*   SN 383535

The nave and chancel have medieval walling but no ancient features. A fine 13th century font with four masks has been removed to the 19th century church of St Llawddog at Cenarth in Carmarthenshire.

LLANWENOG   *Dedication Unknown*   SN 494456

It was under patronage of Sir Rhys Ap Thomas in c1485-90 that a 13th century single chamber with one 14th century south window was given a west tower with a battered plinth and NE stair turret, a coved wagon roof and a new east window, plus a south chapel with communication with the main body by two arches cut through the wall. A Norman scalloped font lies within the south chapel.

LLANWNEN   *Dedication Unknown*   SN 533473

The nave has a round arched south doorway and may be Norman. The tower is 15th century and the chancel may be 13th century although it retains no ancient features.

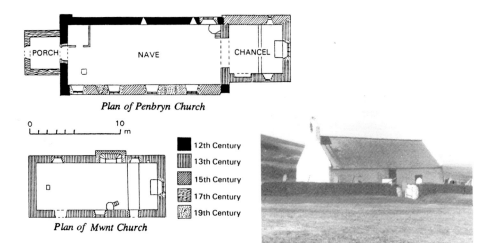

Plan of Penbryn Church

■	12th Century
▦	13th Century
▨	15th Century
▤	17th Century
▦	19th Century

Plan of Mwnt Church

Mwnt Church

MWNT   *Holy Cross*   SN 195520

A scalloped Norman font lies in the 13th or 14th century single chamber delightfully situated on the neck of a coastal headland. A projection in the north wall contains a stair to the former rood loft. The doorways are the only ancient openings, although the wooden framed north windows are pre-Victorian.

Tregaron Church

PENBRYN   *St Michael*   SN 294522

A 17th century west porch and 13th century doorway lead into a nave which is at least partly Norman, having two small windows in the north wall. The chancel and chancel arch were added in the 13th century. In the 15th century the chancel was widened slightly to the north and the nave south wall rebuilt, the windows and arch-braced roof with trefoils over collar-beams being of that period.

STRATA FLORIDA   *St Mary*   SN 746658

A pulpit of 1724 lies in a church dating from 1815 in its present form. The mid 14th century poet Dafydd Ap Gwilym lies buried below a yew tree in the churchyard.

TREGARON   *St Mary*   SN 680597

The 19th century rebuilding left only the fine 14th century west tower with a NE stair turret, a corbelled parapet and an original west window.

The following churches are ancient foundations but have been rebuilt and lack any ancient features: Aberaeron, Betws Ifan, Blaen Pennal, Ciliau Aeron, Gartheli, Llanafon, Llanbardarn Trefeglws, Llandeiniol, Llandre, Llandygwydd, Llangeitho, Llangybi.

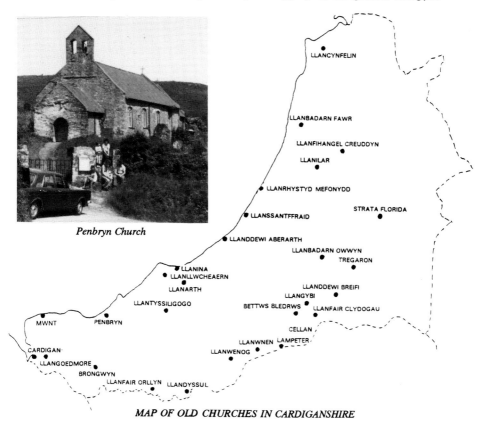

Penbryn Church

MAP OF OLD CHURCHES IN CARDIGANSHIRE

GAZETTEER OF CHURCHES IN CARMARTHENSHIRE

ABERGWILI *St David* SN 440209

Until rebuilt in 1843 the church was double-naved with a row of octagonal piers. The broken cross-slab may be of Bishop Beck, d1293, who founded a college here.

ABERNANT *St Lucia* SN 340241

The nave and chancel each have one small 13th century north window. There is a squint on the south side of the chancel arch. There was a rebuilding in 1706, but the vestry, west porch, and the other windows are all Victorian. The font is 17th century.

BETWS *St David* SN 632117

The nave, porch, and chancel may all be 14th century, the likely date of the south doorway. There was considerable rebuilding in 1872 and a north vestry was added.

CAEO *St Cynwyl* SN 675399

The large west tower with a NE staircase turret dates from c1500. Of about the same period is the wide south aisle with original windows in the end walls and three plain pointed arches towards the nave, the eastern pier being wider than the other two. The furnishings include a 15th century font and an 18th century chest.

CAPEL BEGEWDIN *Dedication Unknown* NS 498147

The R.C.A.H.M. inventory reports the end walls of a well chapel in Llanddarog parish as still standing. The west wall had a 15th century window over an older doorway.

CAPEL BETWS *Dedication Unknown* SN 309267

The wide single chamber is probably medieval but has no old features.

CAPEL BETWS *Dedication Unknown* SN 278284

This is a small overgrown ruin with lancet windows. It consists of a nave, chancel, and a north aisle with a two bay arcade and a squint. Regular services at this remote spot ceased in 1710.

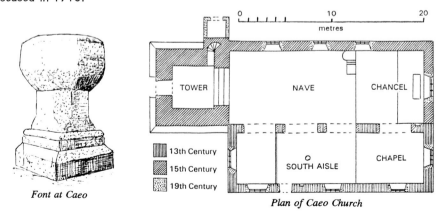

Font at Caeo

Plan of Caeo Church

CAPEL DEWI *St David* SN 659178

Just earthworks mark out the nave, chancel, and porch, plus the priest's house nearby.

CARMARTHEN *St Peter* SN 407200

This is a large church with a west tower having a NE stair turret, a long nave with a south aisle and a north transept (known as the Mayor's Chapel), and a chancel flanked by a south chapel and north vestries. No original openings survive although there are four recesses in the nave north wall. Much of the walling is medieval and it seems that a new 13th century nave and chancel were added to a 12th century nave which then became an aisle. A chantry was founded in the church in the 1390s. The fine tomb of Sir Rhys ap Thomas has come from the church of the nearby Franciscan Friary. In the chancel are a wall monument to Anne, Lady Vaughan, d1672 and an organ built for, but rejected by, King George III.

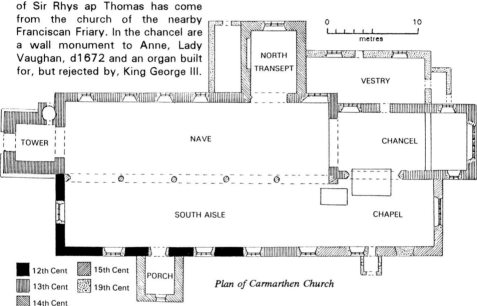

Plan of Carmarthen Church

St Peter's Church, Carmarthen

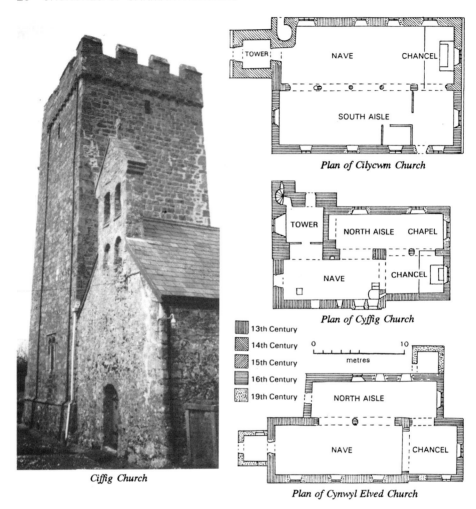

Plan of Cilycwm Church

Plan of Cyffig Church

13th Century
14th Century
15th Century
16th Century
19th Century

0   10

metres

Plan of Cynwyl Elved Church

Ciffig Church

CASTELL DWYRAN *Dedication Unknown* SN 145183

Only after the Reformation did the chapel here assume the status of a parish church.
The 13th century single chamber was mostly rebuilt in 1876 above the foundations
except for the west doorway and the small chancel, transepts, and the porch then
added. The font and stoup may be 13th century. The building is now derelict.

CIFFIG *St Cyffig* SN 208139

The church is dwarfed by its huge NW tower of c1500 with a NE stair turret and a
second storey fitted out with a fireplace for possibly accommodating the priest. The
aisle east of the tower has been added to a 12th or 13th century nave. The aisle
continues into a 16th century chapel with a pair of four-centred arches opening
towards the chancel, which was rebuilt in that period. There is a single similar arch
between the nave and aisle. The font is 13th century but has been re-cut.

CILYCWM *St Michael* SN 753400

This church was probably built shortly after 1291 as it does not appear on a list of churches made that year. By the end of the 14th century a west tower had been added. It has a vaulted basement serving as a porch and a NE stair turret projecting entirely within the nave. The west doorway is 15th century. The south aisle with a five bay arcade was added in the 15th century. The date 1906 appearing over the priest's doorway must refer to a restoration.

CYNWYL ELVED *St Cynwyl* SN 374275

The nave is 14th century like the font and the mutilated stoup at the west end but it has been considerably rebuilt. In the 16th century a new chancel and north aisle were added. The chapel has several original square headed windows with round arched lights and two blocked openings probably of the 18th century.

EGLWYSCYMYN *St Margaret* SN 232107

The western half remains of a vaulted and thick walled 13th century single chamber. One original NE lancet survives. The blocked original doorway lies west of the existing entrance with a 15th century vaulted porch. The chancel was rebuilt in the 19th century. The font is medieval and there is an Ogham stone. There are traces of 13th and 15th century murals and a later set of Commandments in Welsh and English.

EGLWYS FAIR A CHURIG *St Mary & St Curig* SN 190371

The nave and chancel date only from 1770 but contain an older font and a 17th century tomb slab depicting the top half of a male nude.

EGREMONT *St Michael* SN 093203

The church was rebuilt in 1839 but was decayed again by 1917. It contains an early font and a tie beam dated 1782 but probably actually of the 16th century.

HENLLAN FALLTEG
Dedication Unknown SN 185208

The nave has medieval masonry. The rest is all Victorian.

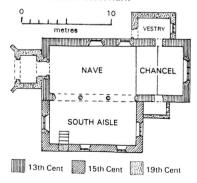

Plan of Llandyfeisant Church

Llandyfeisant Church

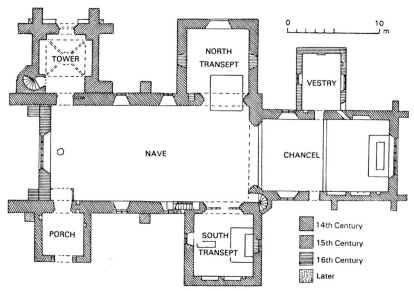

0   10
           m

NORTH TRANSEPT

TOWER

VESTRY

NAVE

CHANCEL

PORCH

SOUTH TRANSEPT

14th Century
15th Century
16th Century
Later

Plan of Kidwelly Church

Kidwelly Church

KIDWELLY *St Mary* SN 408068

The church served a Benedictine Priory founded c1130 although its layout is more that of a large parish church. As rebuilt in the 14th century it comprised a long and wide nave with transepts, a south porch, and a chancel. A porch-tower with a broach spire was added on the north side of the nave c1400. The chancel has fine original windows and a squint from a contemporary vestry on the north side. There are sedilia in the south wall. The siting of a staircase to the rood loft west of the south transept suggests that the eastern part of the nave was divided off by a screen separating the monastic eastern parts from the parochial western two thirds of the nave. After the priory was dissolved the western end nave was shortened, a new west wall being built between the two porches. The south transept has a tablet recording that it was rebuilt in 1767. The rest of the church was restored in 1854. Over the high altar is a 14th century figure of the Virgin. The organ is mid 18th century. The tomb labelled "Ysolda" is probably that of Hawys de Chaworth, d1274. In the south transept is an effigy of a civilian. There is also a 15th century cross-slab.

LAUGHARNE *St Martin* SN 302114

This is a 14th century building of some size with a central tower and boldly projecting buttresses. The south transept has a piscina and a squint and the chancel has a piscina and sedilia. The two porches, the vestries, and most of the windows are of 1873 when foundations were discovered of a smaller earlier nave. The stained glass making the interior dark is also Victorian except for the arms of Sir Guido de Brian in a chancel north window. His effigy once lay in the chancel. There are many memorial tablets plus a 10th or 11th century cross-slab and a fine late medieval cope. The Mariners' Chapel near the castle has two tomb recesses in the north wall. The south wall has gone.

Laugharne Church

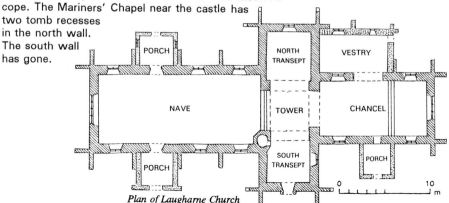

Plan of Laugharne Church

LLANARTHNEY   *St David*   SN 534203

An early nave and a 16th century south aisle were thrown into one in 1826. The west tower is 15th century. It contains a 12th century cross-slab with an inscription.

LLANBOIDY   *St Brynach*   SN 216232

The nave has a blocked 13th century south doorway. The unequally projecting transepts may be 14th century. The chancel and north chapel were entirely rebuilt in the 19th century but reset on the chancel east wall is a 15th century shield with the Dynevor family arms from Whitland Abbey. An early incised slab lies in the south wall.

LLANDAWKE   *St Margaret*   SN 282112

The 13th century nave and chancel have a round arch between them. The font is older, being Norman. The pyramidal roofed west tower with the walls battered up to a considerable height is probably late 13th century. There are two fine 14th century windows in the chancel and another in the nave. Two other windows are 15th century whilst the south doorway could be either 14th or 15th century. The late 14th century female effigy in the chancel is thought to be Margaret, daughter of Robert Marlos.

LLANDDEUSSANT   *St Simon & St Jude*   SN 777245

This is a double-naved church with a four bay arcade. Much of it may be 14th century, the period of the font, but those windows which are not restored are 16th century. West of the south nave is a slightly higher and later chamber probably intended to support or contain a timber framed belfry.

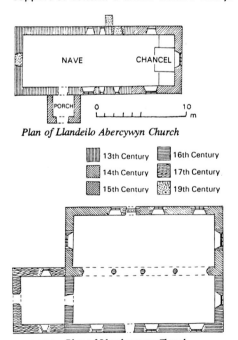

Plan of Llandeilo Abercywyn Church

13th Century		16th Century
14th Century		17th Century
15th Century		19th Century

Plan of Llandeussant Church

Llanddowror Church

LLANDDOWROR   *St Teilo*   SN 256146

The church was entirely rebuilt in 1865 except for the west tower with a SE stair turret. The tower is probably a 16th century rebuilding of an earlier structure. There is an octagonal font decorated with quatrefoils.

LLANDEILO   *St Teilo*   SN 629222

Only the 13th century west tower and an old font survived the rebuilding of 1848-51 by Sir G.G.Scott. The north aisle is now partitioned off as a hall. There are two 10th or 11th century cross-slabs.

LLANDEILO ABERCYWYN   *St Teilo*   SN 309130

The ruined single chamber in a field below a farm is was built by the patron Richard de Londres in the 13th century. It has twin west lancets over a blocked doorway. It was extended eastward and given a south porch c1500. There are stepped internal east buttresses. In 1917 the church was still roofed and had a three-decker pulpit.

LLANDINGAT (LLANDOVERY)   *St Dingad*   SN 770352

The west tower with a NE stair turret, the wide south aisle, the chancel arch, and the east windows are 15th century. The original large single chamber, probably 13th century, was extended eastward before the late medieval remodelling, as the walls at that end have a battered base. The Victorians provided a new arcade and north porch, the latter replacing a two storey structure. They also encased the original font.

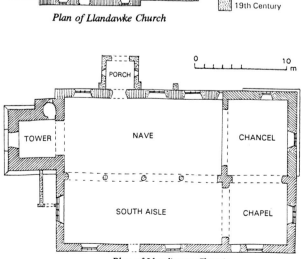

13th Century
14th Century
15th Century
19th Century

Plan of Llandawke Church

Plan of Llandingat Church

Llandingat Church

Llandybie Church

LLANDYBIE *St Tybie* SN 618155

The nave, chancel, aisle, and wide south chapel all have medieval masonry but no datable features. What is now the nave was probably originally a late 14th century north aisle. The 16th century tower lies in a SW corner position projecting slightly west of the nave and south of the aisle. The dates 1823, 1891, and 1968 upon the tower refer to repairs. Coved ceilings were provided c1700 but that in the chancel was removed c1900. There is a monument to Sir Henry Vaughan of Derwydd, d1676.

LLANDYFAELOG *St Tyfaelog* SN 414119

In the 14th century transepts were added to the 13th century nave and chancel. The south transept retains its original east window. The west porch and doorway and the north chapel with a two bay arcade to the chancel are 15th century. The south porch is of uncertain date. The chancel arch is flanked by blocked openings high up.

LLANDYFEISANT (DYNEVOR) *St Teilo* SN 626222

In the 15th century the original 13th century single chamber was given a new east window and a wide south aisle. The three bay arcade was renewed in the 19th century when the west porch and vestry were added. The font is probably 17th century. A piscina has been hollowed out of a 13th century capital, perhaps imported.

LLANEDI *St Edith* SN 589067

Most of the church was rebuilt in 1860 but the tower base with a blocked west doorway may be 13th century and the north chapel is perhaps of c1800.

LLANEGWAD *St Egwad* SN 519214

A stone over the north porch outer arch tells us that the church was rebuilt in 1849. It is a double naved building with a NW tower by the porch but only the north nave now has medieval masonry. The arch heads of the west window look original.

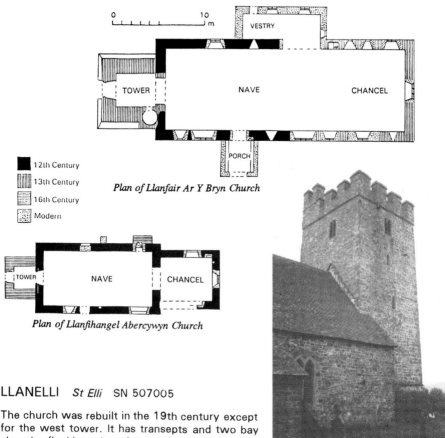

0   10
m

■ 12th Century

▨ 13th Century

▤ 16th Century

▨ Modern

Plan of Llanfair Ar Y Bryn Church

Plan of Llanfihangel Abercywyn Church

Llanfair Ar Y Bryn Church

LLANELLI   *St Elli*   SN 507005

The church was rebuilt in the 19th century except for the west tower. It has transepts and two bay chapels flanking the chancel but the nave is unaisled. See the picture on page 14.

LLANFAIR AR Y BRYN (LLANDOVERY)   *St Mary*   SN 764341

The church is a large single chamber with a west tower remodelled in the 15th century. Norman windows survive in each side wall. The eastern part is probably 13th century as it has windows of that period and of the 14th and 15th centuries. Bricks from the surrounding Roman fort are re-used in the east wall. All that survives of a late 13th or early 14th century SE chapel is a blocked pointed arch in the main south wall.

LLANFIHANGEL ABERCYWYN   *St Michael*   SN 303134

The old church ruin lies some distance from any public road but is worth a visit. The nave and chancel are both probably Norman, the arch between them and the south doorway both being round headed. A Norman font has been removed to the new church of 1847. The 13th century west doorway now opens into a tower of c1500. The chancel has a 15th century east window. A fine set of six late 12th and early 13th century grave-slabs, possibly of pilgrims on their way to St Davids but more probably lords of the adjacent castle mound, lie nearby in the overgrown graveyard.

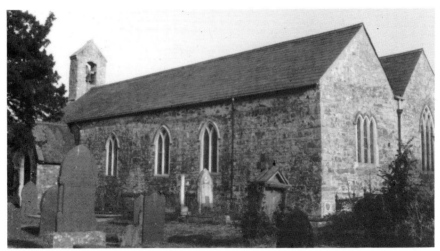

Llanfihangel Ar Arth Church

LLANFIHANGEL AR ARTH *St Michael* SN 456399

The nave with battered walls and the chancel arch are probably 13th century. The chancel is likely to have been widened to the south in the 16th century when an undivided south aisle and chapel each with two arches to the nave and chancel respectively was added. The font is probably 16th or 17th century. There are two Early Christian stones, one with an inscription, the other with crosses.

LLANFIHANGEL CROESFEINI *St Michael* SN 395238

Nothing now remains of this chapel. The name Croesfeini refers to two cross slabs found here which are now in Carmarthen Museum.

LLANFIHANGEL RHOS-Y-CORN *St Michael* SN 529340

A 13th century single chamber was extended eastward soon after. In the 16th century a south aisle was added with an arcade of three plain four-centred arches. The west porch is of uncertain date. The blue-washed font is probably 17th century.

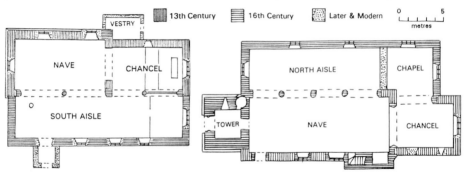

Plan of Llanfihangel Ar Arth Church   *Plan of Llanfynydd Church*

LLANFYNYDD   *St Egwad*   SN 558287

Most of the features of the church are 16th century although the walling of the nave and chancel is 13th century and there is a stoup with a cusped head. There are an embattled west tower, a north aisle with a four bay arcade, and a square Lady Chapel in which is an old chest. At the nave SE corner is a recess with the stair to the former roodloft rising up over up from immediately to the west. Evidence of a major fire was found in the restoration of 1861. There is an old oak chest.

LLANGADOG   *St David*   SN 707285

This cruciform church with a 15th century west tower was restored from ruin in 1889, the south transept being rebuilt and the windows all replaced. There is an old font. Foundations of an apse were discovered. There was a crude Doom mural painting.

LLANGATHEN   *St Cathen*   SN 584221

The church may once have been cruciform with 14th century transepts added to a 13th century nave and chancel. However the north transept is of c1500 in its present state. Also of that period are the wide south aisle with a tomb recess in the outer wall, and the west tower with a corbelled parapet. The south chapel was built c1600 by Bishop Rudd whose huge tomb was erected within it in 1616. The medieval font lies beside a much more modern one. The communion table is late 16th century. There are effigies of a man and woman. A Norman font has been brought in from elsewhere.

LLANGENNECH   *St Cennech*   SN 561019

The church was been rebuilt but retains a 15th century font.

LLANGLYDWEN   *St Clydwen*   SN 175266

A 13th century font lies in the 19th century church.

Llangynnor Church

Llangyndeyrn Church

Llanllwch Church

LLANGYNDEYRN *St Cyndeyrn* SN 456140 & 465126

The tower has a high vault and the unusual feature of a straight stair in the south wall. It is 13th century but was partly rebuilt in 1884. The south doorway and porch are 15th century. Contemporary with them or with the 16th century wide north aisle and north chapel is the south projection containing a roodloft staircase. There is a blocked north doorway. The piscina in the chancel is original. The plain chest is dated 1699. There is a tomb slab in the porch. Not far away lies the ruined 13th century Capel Llyddgen. The west tower is the best preserved part of it.

LLANGYNIN *St Cynin* SN 250198

The nave, north transept, and chancel are likely to be 13th century, and the west tower is not much later. A south aisle was created in the 15th century, probably by extending a former south transept to the west. The east window is 14th century but the other windows have all been renewed.

LLANGYNNOR *St Cynnor* SN 430203

The nave and chancel are 13th century. The west porch is 15th or 16th century and the north aisle and north chapel are 16th or 17th century. The arcade to the nave is Victorian but two old arches of a very rustic type divide the chapel from the chancel.

LLANGYNOG *St Cynog* SN 340163

This building ranked only as a chapel-of-ease to Llanstephen until 1879. The nave and chancel are both probably 13th century although the only feature likely to be that old is the west doorway. The south aisle with three four-centred arches to the nave and one more towards the chancel is probably 16th century.

Llanpumpsaint Church

Llanllwni Church

LLANLLAWDOG
St Llawdog   SN 458295

A font probably of the 17th century lies in the 19th century church.

LLANLLWCH
St Mary   SN 385188

A rock faced Victorian north aisle has a higher roof than that of the nave. There are traces of a former south doorway below one of the south windows, but the west tower is the chief medieval relic. It has a stair projection corbelled out above the plinth and not continued up at the top as a turret.

LLANLLWNI   *St Llwni*   SN 473413

The tower, nave and chancel all have 13th century walls but the only ancient features are a blocked arch in the chancel north wall and an altar stone by the west door.

LLANON   *St Non*   SN 540084

The nave and chancel are 13th century. The tower is probably also of that period but was remodelled when the south aisle was added at the end of the medieval period. The arcade was taken out and a flat ceiling inserted in the early 19th century.

LLANPUMPSAINT   *SS Ceitho, Celynnin, Gwyn, Gwyno, & Gwynoro*   SN 418291

The chancel with one original north lancet may be a later addition to the nave which is on a different axis. Otherwise the features are of 1882. An altar stone from an oratory in the churchyard now lies inside the church, whilst a cross-slab still lies outside. A day school was held in a west gallery until 1862.

LLANSADWRN *St Sadwrn* SN 695315

The chancel NE window looks Norman but may be late medieval. The nave south doorway is 13th century and has a 14th century porch in front of it. The 16th century Abermarlais chapel on the south side contains an old chest and has one arch to each of the nave and chancel. Its east window is partly blocked. The chancel arch is Victorian. The font is 15th century, the pulpit is old, and there is an ancient stoup.

LLANSADYRNIN *St Sadyrnin* SN 282103

The church itself is of 1859 but there is a cusped medieval niche with pinnacles fixed on the east wall and a churchyard cross shaft supporting a sundial dated 1805.

LLANSAWEL *St Sawyl* SN 621363

There are late 14th century windows in the east end of the nave and the chancel which inclines slightly to the north and contains an Easter Sepulchre. The 15th century west tower has a NE stair turret. The chest in the vestry is dated 1757.

LLANSTEPHEN *St Stephen* SN 350108

The nave and the quadripartite vaulted west tower with a NE stair turret are of the same period as the castle i.e. 13th century. The chancel and transepts are 14th century. The north transept has a squint. Probably all of the 16th century are the nave wagon roof, the south porch, the chancel east window, and the Laques Chapel with a two bay arcade on the north side of the chancel. The chapel contains a scalloped Norman font and a monument to David Lloyd, d1670, and his wife.

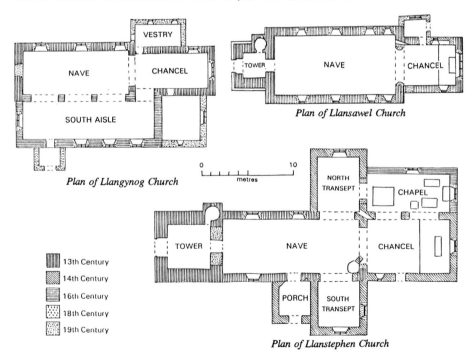

Plan of Llangynog Church

Plan of Llansawel Church

Plan of Llanstephen Church

13th Century
14th Century
16th Century
18th Century
19th Century

Llanybydder Church

Llanstephen Church

LLANWRDA   *St Cawrdaf*   SN 713319

The original single chamber has medieval walling and contains an old font and a stoup. The north aisle and vestry and all the windows are Victorian.

LLANYBRI   *St Mary*   SN 335125

The Marbell Chapel in the middle of Llanybri village was a chapel-of-ease to Llanstephen until the 17th century. It was sold to Nonconformist Dissenters in the 18th century. Since the early 20th century it has become a ruin, the side walls of the single chamber being now reduced to waist level. The east wall with a late 16th century window, and the west tower with a pointed tunnel vault and pyramidal roof stand higher. The tower was embattled until rebuilt after a fire in the 19th century.

LLANYBYDDER   *St Peter*   SN 519439

This church was in a poor condition in 1710 but was restored in 1885. The west tower with a NE stair turret and a corbelled parapet is 16th century. The nave and chancel have no old features save a cusped north lancet to light the former screen. The old font is broken and a stoup has been used instead for baptisms.

LLANYCRWYS   *St David*   SN 645454

The single chamber has been most rebuilt above the foundations. The renewed west doorway suggests a 14th century date. The font may be 17th century. There is a plain old oak chest. In the vestry is a fragment of an oak beam dated 1663.

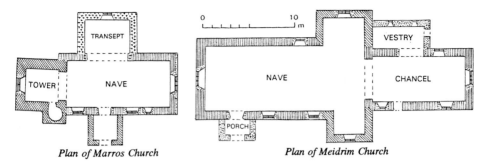

Plan of Marros Church   Plan of Meidrim Church

MARROS *St Lawrence* SN 208089

A 14th century west tower and vaulted south porch with a stoup have been added to a small 13th century chamber. The tower formed an important landmark for sailors and has an upper room with a fireplace once used as a school. Since the turret stair doorway was closed in 1844 access to the top has been via a hole in the vault. The north transept is probably 18th century. The church was partly rebuilt in 1844.

MEIDRIM *St David* SN 289210

The long nave and chancel are probably 13th century but were mostly rebuilt above the foundations in the late 19th century. Their only ancient surviving feature is the priest's doorway. The shallow transepts were probably added in the 14th century which is the period to which the font belongs.

MERTHYR *St Enfael* SN 352208

The Victorian church contains an old font and has an inscribed stone in the porch.

Myddvai Church

MYDDVAI
St Michael SN773302

In the late 15th century a north aisle and chapel were added to a 13th century barrel-vaulted nave and chancel. The chancel south wall has a corbel table, There are several old windows, but the large south windows and the west windows are Victorian. There is blocked north doorway. The font basin with four lugs has been brought here from the vanished chapel of Dol Hywell.

PEMBREY
St Illtud SN 429011

The church existed by 1120 when it was given to Sherborne Abbey, and a scalloped font survived until 1857. A wide new north aisle with an arcade of four-centred arches, a north chapel, and a tower with double stepped battlements west of the aisle were added in the 14th century to a 13th century nave and chancel. Of the 16th century are the nave and chancel roofs and some stained glass in a south window with the Lancaster Arms and the Emblems of The Passion. The south doorway is dated 1717.

PENCARREG
St Patrick SN 535450

In the church of 1878 is a Norman font bowl with four carved heads thought to represent Christ as a youth, as a man, as the Crucified One, and the Glorified One.

PENDINE
St Margaret SN 228088

Only a seven sided 14th century font and the small 16th or 17th century tower survived the rebuilding of 1869 when a round arch between nave and chancel was replaced. The church was "out of repair" in 1672.

Pembrey Church

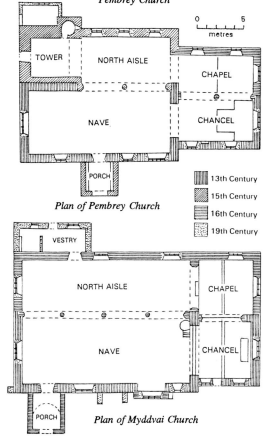

Plan of Pembrey Church

TOWER NORTH AISLE CHAPEL NAVE CHANCEL PORCH

0   5
metres

IIIII 13th Century
//// 15th Century
≡≡≡≡ 16th Century
:::: 19th Century

VESTRY NORTH AISLE CHAPEL NAVE CHANCEL PORCH

Plan of Myddvai Church

ST CLEARS   *St Mary Magdalene*   SN 281148

The large and massively walled nave and chancel with a fine arch between them are Norman. They served a Cluniac priory founded c1120 and suppressed along with other alien priories dependent on French abbeys during Henry V's wars against the French. The west tower with a high barrel vault is 13th century. A blocked nave south doorway matches that in the tower west wall. All the windows are Victorian. There is an old font. The oldest monument is the tablet to Vicar Timothy Powell, d1719.

ST ISHMAELS   *St Ishmael*   SN 363084 & 385080

The font is Norman and so perhaps is the nave. The chancel with a bench all around it and the south transept with a squint are 13th century. The porch continued up as a saddle-back roofed tower and the arcade to the north aisle may be 14th century. Access to the belfry is only by a ladder as there is no staircase. All the windows are of 1860. The church at Llansaint has a small nave and chancel which may be Norman, and a later west tower. It was a chapel-of-ease to St Ishmael's. There was another church nearby at Hawton.

TALLEY   *St Mary*   SN 633228

At the Reformation a parish church was made by walling off the transepts, aisles, and west half of the nave of the 12th and 13th century abbey church, and providing a small new chancel within the monastic one. The windows had no glass in 1705 as the parish was said to be poor. A new church nearby was provided in 1772 and replaced in the 19th century.

The following churches have been rebuilt and lack any ancient features: Llandarog, Llanfihangel Cilfargen, Llangeller, Llanwinio, Newchurch, Penboyr.

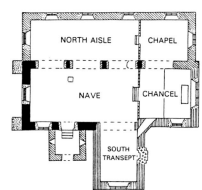

Plan of St Ishmaels Church

0		10		20

metres

■ 12th Century ▨ 14th Century
▥ 13th Century ▨ 15th Century
▧ Later & Modern

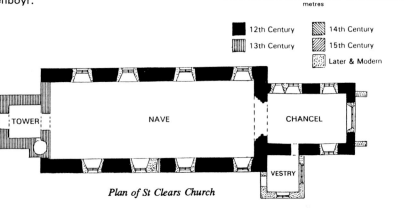

Plan of St Clears Church

St Ishmaels Church

MAP OF OLD CHURCHES IN CARMARTHENSHIRE

GAZETTEER OF PEMBROKESHIRE CHURCHES

AMBLESTON *St Mary* SN 001258

The low 15th century west tower with a vault and spire was repaired in 1779. The 13th century nave and chancel were mostly rebuilt in 1906. There is a Norman font.

AMROTH *St Elidyr* SN 164078

The nave and chancel are probably of c1200 but the arch between them is Victorian. The nave has a pointed barrel-vault and a western extension of 1855 when a south porch was added. The north transeptal tower and north chapel are of c1500 and there are blocked arches from the chancel and south transept to former south chapel of the same date. There is a Norman font with leaves carved upon it.

ANGLE *St Mary* SR 867029

The nave north wall and the north transept are probably 13th century, and the font is Norman. The 15th century tower has a vaulted lowest stage and a dome-roofed belfry. The nave south wall, the porch, chancel, and north chapel are all Victorian. The nearby chapel of St Anthony is a small single chamber over a vault built in 1447 by Edward de Shirburn. A tomb recess lies empty on one side, and a priest's effigy on the other.

Amroth Church   *Angle Church*

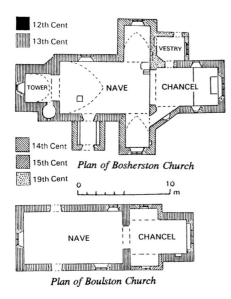

Plan of Bosherston Church

■ 12th Cent

▒ 13th Cent

▨ 14th Cent

▨ 15th Cent

░ 19th Cent

VESTRY

TOWER   NAVE   CHANCEL

0   10
└─────────────┘ m

NAVE   CHANCEL

Plan of Boulston Church

Boulston Church

BAYVIL   *St Andrew*   SN 102406

This disused medieval single chamber without external features of interest has a good Georgian interior including a three decker pulpit.

BEGELLY   *St Mary*   SN 118073

The 14th century north chapel has two arches to the chancel and one to the nave. The nave, chancel, and small south transept with a squint are all probably 13th century. The lofty vaulted west tower is probably 16th century but the battlements are later.

BLETHERSTON   *St Mary*   SN 070212

There is an Easter Sepulchre in the chancel north wall. Much of the walling may be 13th century like the pentagonal font, but the west doorway and the south aisle with a doorway and a three bay arcade are early 16th century.

BOULSTON   *Dedication Unknown*

Despite being heavily restored in 1843 the 13th century nave and chancel divided by a plain pointed arch now lie in ruins. They are hidden away in vegetation near the shore far from any road. The recesses in the chancel were for Wogan family tombs.

BOSHERSTON   *St Michael*   SR 966948

The south transept has a squint and contains a crudely made figure, whilst the north transept contains an effigy of a veiled lady with a dog at her feet. Both transepts have 14th century ogival headed piscinae and pointed tunnel-vaults like that of the probably slightly earlier nave. There are corbels for a rood beam across the chancel arch but the arch itself has been renewed. The west tower has a round arched vault. The font is Norman. There is part of a re-erected churchyard cross.

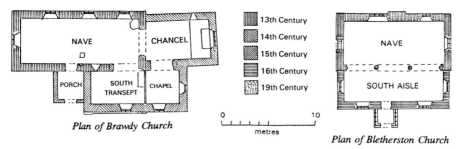

13th Century
14th Century
15th Century
16th Century
19th Century

Plan of Brawdy Church

0 _____ 10
metres

Plan of Bletherston Church

BRAWDY   *St David*   SM 857241

The nave walls with one crudely made south lancet without glass and the font are of c1200. A pointed arch opens into a chancel of c1300 inclined to the north. A similar arch gives onto a small 13th century transept enlarged to the west in the early 15th century when the Rice Chapel was added east of it. There is a fragment of an inscribed stone in the nave and in the porch are three old stones, two with Ogham inscriptions.

BRIDELL   *St David*   SN 176421

Little apart from the west wall and font survived the restoration of 1886.

BURTON   *St Mary*   SM 985056

The small transepts are 14th century additions to a 13th century nave and chancel. The west tower and probably also the porch are 15th or 16th century. The north aisle are Victorian and the chapel of St Andrew on the south side has been rebuilt. In the nave is a tomb of c1520 of one of the Wogans of Milton and Boulston. There is no effigy. The chancel has a piscina, a recess, and a squint from the south transept.

Burton Church

Chancel, Carew Cheriton,

Cleydai Church

Tower, Carew Cheriton

CAMROSE   *St Ismael*   SM 928200

A scalloped Norman font lies in the long nave which has a rood-loft stair on the north side and a 15th century south doorway. The chancel has a blocked 13th century lancet, a 14th century piscina, and a 15th century south window. A 14th century south chapel has been demolished and the single arches to the nave and chancel blocked up. The thin west tower is of uncertain date. The nave windows are of 1883.

CAREW CHERITON   *St Mary*   SS 046028

This church is larger and more typically English than its neighbours. The late 13th century chancel has three sedilia and buttresses. There are recesses containing the effigies of a 14th century priest, a girl under a canopy, and Sir Nicholas Carew, d1311. There is also a monument to Sir John Carew, d1637, and his wife Elizabeth. The tiles of c1500 around the sanctuary are said to have come from the nearby castle. The north window and vestry with a squint towards the altar are 14th century, as are the aisles with two bay arcades. The chancel arch and transept arches are 15th century. The tower and porch are of c1500. The end bay of the north transept is later.

CASTELLAN   *Dedication Unknown*   SN 190360 approx

Not much of this building now stands above the foundations.

CASTLEBYTHE   *St Michael*   SN 021210

The plain pointed chancel arch dates from c1200. The chancel was later widened southwards and given a recess on that side. There was much rebuilding in 1875 but the building is now derelict.

CASTLEMARTIN   *St Michael*   SR 911989

The north aisle has a squint to the chancel and an arcade of c1200 with four plain single stepped arches carried on octagonal piers with shafts to the north and south. Two similar blank arches appear in the chancel, which has a blocked south lancet, and it seems that a north chapel and transept have been removed. There was evidently once a south chapel reached by an arch, now blocked, in the east wall of the 13th century transeptal south tower. The tower top is of Tudor date and was once gabled. The vaulted porch is surmounted by a saddle-back roofed belfry. The font is Norman.

CILGERRAN   *St Llawddog*   SN 191431

Only the 13th century west tower and three worn 18th century memorials survived the rebuilding of the church in 1855. There is an Ogham stone outside to the south.

CLYDAI   *St Clydai*   SN 251355

The west tower with a low pointed arch and the stoup inside the north doorway are 13th century. The rood-loft staircase and the south aisle (the Capel Mair) may be 15th century. The porch and the chancel are Victorian, as are all the windows. There are three incised grave-stones, one having a circled cross.

COSHESTON   *St Michael*   SN 001037

The nave, chancel, south transept or Packeston chapel with a tomb recess, and the north aisle with a two bay arcade are all medieval but have no openings predating the 1885 restoration.

CRUNWEAR   *St Elidyr*   SN 186107

Only the vaulted tower with a NE stair turret and a blocked west doorway and the north transept of this 13th century cruciform church have survived unrebuilt.

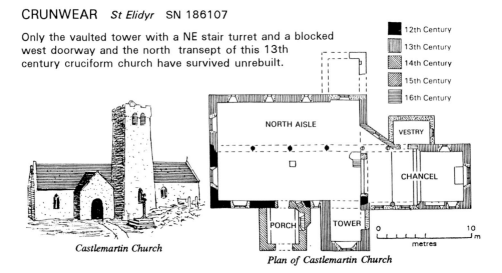

■	12th Century
▦	13th Century
▨	14th Century
▧	15th Century
▤	16th Century

Castlemartin Church

Plan of Castlemartin Church

DALE *St James* SM 806057

The west tower is 15th century. The nave and chancel south walls and their windows are Victorian but the battered east and north walls are medieval.

DINAS *St Brynach* SN 014400

Only the west gable with a 15th century doorway and a fragment of the south wall remain beside the shore. The rest of the church was destroyed in a gale in the autumn of 1859. Old drawings show it as cruciform with a double bellcote on the west gable.

EAST WILLIAMSON *St Elidyr* SN 098049

The narrow 13th century nave and chancel are divided by a plain pointed arch. A small turret is perched on the west wall. The church has been heavily restored.

EGLWYSWRW *St Cristiolis* SN 142385

The church has medieval masonry but the features are of 1829 and 1883 when a north transept was removed. There was once a chapel near the holy well here but it was destroyed by order of Elizabeth I's Privy Council because it was frequented by Catholics.

FLIMSTON *St Martin* SR 924956

In the middle of an army artillery range is a disused vaulted chapel. It served as a barn for many years but was made into a chapel again in 1903.

FRESHWATER EAST *Dedication Unknown* SS 020986

This is a small ruined chapel-of-ease in Lamphrey parish, probably 13th century.

FREYSTROP
St Justinian   SM 956119

The small main body and north transept have a stone roofed squint passage between them but were mostly rebuilt in 1874. The font is probably of c1200.

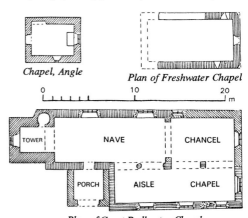

Chapel, Angle

Plan of Freshwater Chapel

GRANSTON
St Catherine   SM 896341

A late 14th century font lies in the church which was rebuilt in 1877.

GREAT RUDBAXTON
St Michael   SM 961206 & 985188

Plan of Great Rudbaxton Church

The long 16th century south chapel east of the older porch has a pair of four-centred arches to each of the 13th century nave and later chancel. The whole of the chapel east wall is filled with a monument to several late 17th century Howards and Pictons. The west tower is 15th century. Little remains of St Leonard's chapel by the castle.

Gumfreston Church

GUMFRESTON   *St Lawrence*   SN 107011

There is a narrow round arch between the Norman nave and chancel. The tiny rib-vaulted south chapel and the transeptal north tower with a squint are late 13th century. The vaulted west porch is later. In the south wall are plain windows of the 17th century and the baptistry recess in the north wall is probably contemporary.

HAROLDSTON   *St Issell*   SM 964140

The nave and bellcote are 13th century. The porch and chancel are later. The chancel is not divided from the nave. A Norman font has survived much restoration.

HAROLDSTON WEST   *St Madoc*   SM 866154

The scalloped font and blocked south doorway date the small nave and chancel to c1200. Most of the rest was renewed in the 19th century.

HASGUARD   *St Peter*   SM 853105

The chancel is all Victorian but the nave has a 13th century north doorway, a slightly later south porch and bellcote, and contains a 14th century font.

Plan of Herbrandston Church

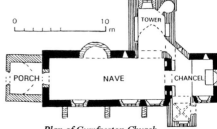

Plan of Gumfreston Church

HAVERFORDWEST *St Martin*

SM 952158

The spacious nave and narrower chancel have old masonry but the triple 14th century sedilia is their only pre-19th century feature. East of the 14th century south porch is a contemporary aisle with a 15th century east window. There is a NW tower with a heavy battered base. In the chancel is a floriated cross-slab.

St Martin's Church, Haverfordwest

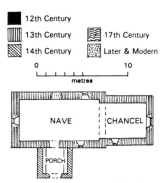

■	12th Century		
⫲	13th Century	≋	17th Century
⧄	14th Century	⣿	Later & Modern

Plan of Haroldston Church

Interior of St Mary's Church Haverfordwest

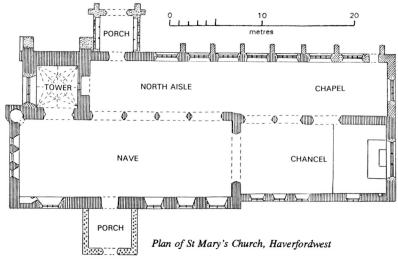

Old postcard of St Mary's Church, Haverfordwest

HAVERFORDWEST *St Mary* SM 953157

The large nave and chancel have several late 13th century windows on the south side and of the same date are the four arches to the nave and another two arches to the chancel from the north aisle plus the north doorway. One pier in the nave has shaft rings. On the chancel arch appear heads representing the Earl of Pembroke and his wife Lady Joan de Clare. The NW tower with a fan-vault, and the clerestory are 15th century, and the north and south porches are 19th and 18th century respectively. There are fine late medieval roofs. The effigy of c1450 has the badge (three scalloped shells) of a pilgrim to Santiago de Compostella in Spain. There is a brass with a kneeling figure of John David, a former Mayor of Haverfordwest, d1651.

Plan of St Mary's Church, Haverfordwest

HAVERFORDWEST   *St Thomas*   SM 955155

The nave and narrow aisle with a seven bay arcade has mostly been rebuilt but the west tower with a cross and two figures on the west side is 13th century, the chancel has old masonry, and there is a 14th century cross-slab inside.

HAYSCASTLE   *St Mary*   SM 896256

The nave and chancel are Norman but the latter has been rebuilt. The font is also Norman. The wooden framed windows are all 19th century.

HENRY'S MOAT   *St Brynach*   SN 045275 & 054280

The nave and chancel are probably 13th century and the south transept is probably 14th century but the restoration of 1884 has left no datable features. In the church is a stone from the nearby chapel which once stood alongside the nearby holy well.

HERBRANDSTON   *St Mary*   SM 871076

The nave and the chancel with tomb recesses on either side are 13th century although the windows are Victorian. One recess contains a damaged 14th century military effigy. The porches are probably 14th century and there is a west tower inclined to the north. See page 52.

HODGESTON   *Dedication Unknown*   SS 030994

The 13th century nave has a pointed tunnel-vault, a scalloped Norman font, and traces of late medieval windows high up. There is a small west tower. The 14th century chancel has a very fine set of sedilia. There was much rebuilding in 1851.

HUBBERSTON
St David   SM 891062

The nave and chancel walls are 13th century. The west tower and two chancel windows are 15th century. The transepts, vestries, and porch are 19th century.

JEFFREYSTON
SS Jeffrey & Oswald   SN 090065

East of the north transept with a squint is a narrow chapel of two bays, whilst west of the transept is a square chapel or vestry. On the south side is another narrow chapel of two bays with a vault. These parts have no datable features. The west tower and vaulted porch are probably 15th century. There were no north windows prior to the Victorian restoration. A churchyard cross lies nearby.

Hodgeston Church

Sedilia at Hodgeston

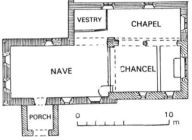

Plan of Llanddewi Velfrey Church

Johnston Church

JOHNSTON *St Peter* SM 933104

Johnston is named after the late 12th century knight John de Rupe, whose son Thomas built the church in the early 13th century. The nave and chancel doorways may be that early. The chancel doorway was soon blocked and two sedilia built against it on the inside. There are tiny transepts and beside them are recesses. A piscina was discovered in the south transept in the restoration of 1908. The chancel has 15th century windows and has a chancel arch with narrow openings either side.

JORDANSTON *St Cawdra* SM 918324

A Norman font survived the total rebuilding of the church in 1797 and 1863.

LAMBSTON *St Ismael* SM 909164

The nave and chancel with a plain pointed arch connecting them plus the font are of c1200. There is a fine old roof and one 15th century north window. There are corbels for a former rood beam. The church was heavily restored in the 1890s.

LAMPHEY *St Tyfei* SM 015004

A Victorian chancel arch now divides the 14th century single wide chamber. The chancel has a piscina and lancets that are partly original but the west tower, the north transept with a squint, and the tiny south transept have no ancient features. The Norman font is carved with scallops, leaves and two cable mouldings.

LAWRENNY *St Caradog* SN 017068

The chancel arch looks Norman but the chancel with several original openings is late 13th century and the transepts and nave doorways are also of that period. The squint between the north transept and chancel has a recess containing the effigy of a cross-legged knight of c1300. There is a double bellcote over the chancel arch but a west tower was added in the 16th century. The porch and vestry are Victorian.

LETTERSTON *St Giles* SM 939296

In the church of 1881 are a 14th century female effigy, a 15th century piscina, and a 15th century hexagonal font with scallops.

LLANBEDR VELFREY *St Peter* SN 153144

The nave and north transept may be 13th century but the chancel has two 14th century windows and there is a 14th century south aisle with a five bay arcade. One south window and the altar tomb of the Phillips's of Lampeter are 17th century.

LLANDDEWI VELFREY *St David* SN 144158

The 13th century nave and the 14th century chancel are much renewed. The 16th century chapel has one arch to the nave and two arches to the chancel.

LLANDEILO LLWYDARTH *St Teilo* SN 099269

Only the lower part of the walls of this remote church now survive although it was roofed until early this century. In a brick pump-house serving the nearby farm is St Teilo's well. The waters were said to be effective as a cure only if drunk early in the morning out of part of a skull which was purchased by bogus museum officials in 1950. It was said to be the skull of the saint himself and has now vanished.

LLANDELOY *St Teilo or Teloi* SM 857266

This church lay in ruins from c1850 until the 1920s, being temporarily superseded by an iron church of 1897. A narrow arch of c1200 divides the nave and narrow chancel and the north doorway is round headed. The chancel south wall is thick enough to contain small rooms. There is a south transept with a low arch to the nave and a squint to the chancel. The former rood-loft staircase now gives access to the pulpit.

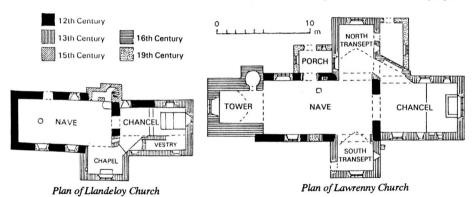

Plan of Llandeloy Church   *Plan of Lawrenny Church*

Derelict church at Llanfihangel Penbedw

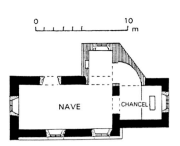

Plan of Llanhywel Church

LLANDISSILIO *St Tyssilio* SN 120218

The nave seems to have been widened as its width now corresponds to that of the chancel and the narrow north vestry or chapel. Except for one 17th century south window and a 15th century top to that next to it all the openings are 19th century. Set in the south wall are two early inscribed stones.

LLANFELLTEG WEST *St Mallteg* SN 147193

The church has been mostly rebuilt. The nave and vaulted north transept are 13th century in origin, whilst the chancel was rebuilt wider later in the medieval period.

LLANFIHANGEL PENBEDW *St Michael* SN 208395

This derelict ivy-grown church with a horse kept in the churchyard has a long narrow nave, a low west tower, a north transept, and a chancel reached through a plain pointed arch. Most of it is 13th century but no pre-19th century openings now survive.

LLANGWM *St Jerome* SM 990094

The nave, chancel, and small barrel-vaulted south transept are 13th century. In c1380 a bigger north transept, the Roch Chapel, was added. It has a two bay arcade with the Barri arms on the pier, two ogival headed recesses in the north wall containing the effigies of a cross-legged knight and lady, and a pillar piscina in the east wall. The church was heavily restored in 1856.

LLANHAWER *St David* SM 987359

The church has been rebuilt but has at one corner a "weeping stone" i.e. spring said to never run dry.

LLANHYWEL *St Hywel* SM 818274

The internally whitewashed nave and chancel with a plain round arch between them are Norman like the scalloped font with slight spurs at the base. The small north transept with a pointed tunnel vault and a very wide squint is probably 13th century.

LLANREITHAN *St Reithan* SM 865284

Only a Norman font survives in the church which was rebuilt in 1858.

LLANRIAN   *St Rhian*   SM 819314

The nave and the west tower (except for the stepped gables to north and south) are 13th century. The chancel is Victorian. The transepts may be post-Reformation.

LLANSTADWELL   *St Tudwal*   SM 955050

The 15th century west tower is very lofty. The nave, the chancel with a piscina and a blocked north lancet, and the north chapel with a squint are probably all 13th century. The walls and floor were raised in 1876 and the windows, porch, south transept, and vestry all date from about that time.

LLANSTINIAN   *St Justinian*   SM 954338

The narrow chancel and the south transept with a squint are covered with pointed tunnel vaults. Probably the walls are 13th century, the chancel arch being a plain pointed opening, but the few narrow windows are all of late date. The font is Norman.

LLANTWYD   *St Twyd*   SN 155419

In the church of 1884 is a fine 14th century cross-slab and in the porch are two old corbels with male heads.

LLANWNDA   *St Gwyndaf*   SM 933396

Much of the church is of 1881. The north aisle containing a roodloft staircase and porch are both vaulted. Features of interest are the two piscinae, the crosses on the chancel walls, and the head of a priest on a 15th century roof beam.

LLANYCEFN   *Ded Unknown*   SN 097237

The church was rebuilt in 1904, a tower having been removed. The font may be 15th century.

LLANYCHAER   *St David*   SM 992345

A Norman font remains in the church of 1876.

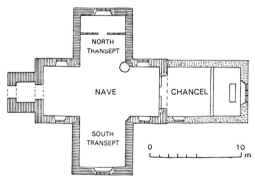

Plan of Llanrian Church

Llanstadwell Church

Loveston Church   *Llawhaden Church*

LLAWHADEN   *St Aedden*   SN 075175 & 066172

A large new nave and chancel were added in the 14th century under patronage of the Bishops of St Davids. In 1862 the nave was mostly rebuilt, the south doorway being blocked and a west porch added. The original 13th century chancel was retained as a south chapel and the original south tower with a stair turret on the west side survives on the south side of the huge lofty new tower raised between it and the new nave. The effigy of a priest lies in a recess in the south chapel, and there is a Norman font. In the village is a lofty vaulted chapel which served a hospital founded by Bishop Beck in 1287. The chapel was dedicated to St Mary, St Thomas and St Edmund.

LLYS-Y-FRAN   *St Meilyr*   SN 039242

A semi-circular baptistry recess has been formed at unknown date to contain the 14th century font. The chancel arch may be Norman.

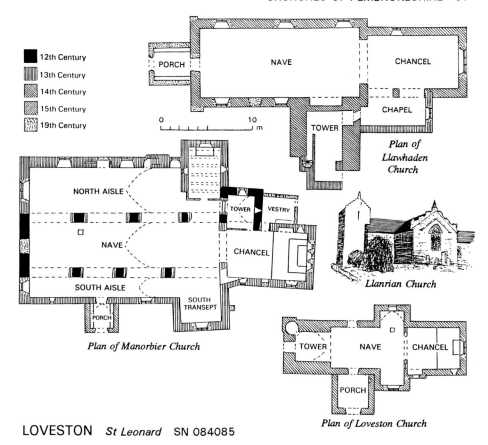

12th Century
13th Century
14th Century
15th Century
19th Century

PORCH NAVE CHANCEL

CHAPEL

TOWER

0   10
        m

Plan of
Llawhaden
Church

NORTH AISLE

NAVE

SOUTH AISLE

TOWER VESTRY

CHANCEL

SOUTH
TRANSEPT

PORCH

Plan of Manorbier Church

Llanrian Church

TOWER NAVE CHANCEL

PORCH

Plan of Loveston Church

LOVESTON *St Leonard* SN 084085

Tiny openings on either side of the chancel arch serve the transepts as squints. The transepts, nave, and the later medieval west tower all have pointed tunnel-vaults. The porch may be 14th century and the chancel is 15th century.

LUDCHURCH *St Elidyr* SN 141109

The nave and chancel are 13th century. The west tower and the south aisle are 16th century. The aisle has three arches on octagonal piers towards the nave and two towards the chancel. One nave pier has a head carved upon the top of it.

MANORBIER *St James* SS 065977

This is a particularly interesting church. To a long narrow Norman nave of which one window remains high up, were added in the early 13th century a new wider chancel, a south transept and narrow south aisle. then a rib-vaulted north transept was added, and at the end of the 13th century a wide north aisle with two light windows was provided. The arcades have plain pointed arches on square piers and the nave, aisles, south transept, and south porch are all covered with pointed tunnel-vaults. The tower set between the chancel and north transept is thought to be Norman. In the north aisle outer wall is a staircase which once led to the loft upon the rood-screen.

Manorbier Church

MANORDEIFI *St David* SN 228432

A modern recess in the outside of the 13th century west tower contains a monument to the Lewis family. The nave and chancel are also 13th century, but the one surviving old window is 15th century. The north wall was rebuilt in the 19th century.

MARLOES *St Peter* SM 793085

The nave containing a Norman font, the vaulted chancel, and the transepts with squints are all 13th century but the east wall and the external openings are renewed.

MARTLETWY *St Marcellus* SN 035106

The chancel south windows and round chancel arch are of c1200. The north aisle with a two bay arcade is 13th century. The north chapel and porch are late medieval.

MINWEAR
St Womar SN 040129

The small nave and chancel and tiny transepts are 13th century. The north chapel with a two bay arcade, the openings either side of the chancel arch, and the belfry raised above the thick west wall are of the 16th and 17th centuries. The four heads on the font probably represent the Four Evangelists.

MILFORD HAVEN
St Thomas Becket SM 910055

Hidden in a back street is a small restored medieval chapel.

Marloes Church

Monkton Church

MONKTON   *St Nicholas*   SR 978014

Originally this long church served a priory with a cloister and domestic buildings to the north. The nave has a pointed tunnel-vault and has a south doorway and porch of c1200. There is a plain tomb chest to Sir Hugh Owen, d1612, and in the south transeptal tower of c1300 is an altar tomb to Sir Francis Meyrike, d1603. The chancel is mostly rebuilt above the level of the sills of the windows. There are two north chapels, the eastern of which has a narrow gap between it and the chancel. In the chancel north wall are recesses with a worn effigy of a priest or lady and the indents of brasses of a kneeling knight of c1500 with his wife, children, saints, and shields.

MOUNTON   *Dedication Unknown*   SN 094119

This neglected single chamber of the 13th or 14th century has a west porch. It was remodelled in the 18th century, one chancel beam being dated 1743.

MYNACHLOG DDU   *St Dogmael*   SN 132283

This disused church has a main body probably of the 13th century with a 15th century south aisle with a three bay arcade on octagonal piers.

Plan of Minwear Church

0 ⌞⌟⌞⌟⌞⌟⌞⌟⌞⌟ 10 m

■ 12th Century
▨ 13th Century
▧ 14th Century
▨ 15th Century
▨ 17th Century
▨ 19th Century

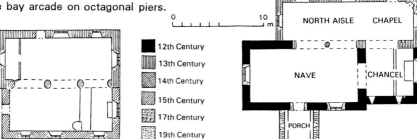

Plan of Mynachlog Ddu Church

Plan of Martletwy Church

Nevern Church

Narberth Church

NARBERTH   *St Andrew*   SN 108144

The church was heavily restored in 1879. Only the north transeptal tower, the north wall of the wide nave, and the large north chapel are likely to be medieval.

NEVERN   *St Brynach*   SN 083401

The long nave and chancel may be all of the 15th century as no features are earlier than that. There are transeptal chapels on each side, that on the south being rib-vaulted in two bays. The pier and two arches are Victorian insertions below a wider, flatter original single arch. Two chapel windows have an Ogham stone and another tomb-stone as sills. The west tower is 16th century. Some restoration was carried out in 1863. South of the church is a very fine Celtic cross of c1000.

NEWGALE   *St Caradoc*   SM 854209

Just a faint hollow now marks the site of this small chapel. In the early 19th century Richard Fenton described it as long and narrow and built of beach pebbles and mortar.

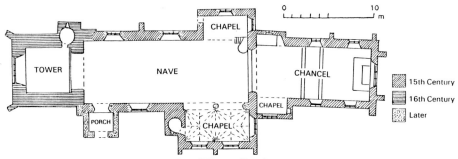

Plan of Nevern Church

NEW MOAT *St Nicholas* SN 062253

The tower is old but the nave, north aisle, chancel, and north chapel were rebuilt in the 19th century. There is an altar tomb of William Scourfield, d1621.

NEWPORT *St Mary* SN 058389

The west tower is 16th century. The chancel and nave have old masonry but no old features, although the nave is flanked by two bay chapels (or aisled transepts). There are fragments of a 14th century cross-slab. The communion table is 17th century.

NEWTON NORTH *Dedication Unknown* SM 066133

The pointed chancel arch on simple imposts dates the nave and chancel to c1200. The west tower and north windows are 16th century. The church was a ruin c1910.

NOLTON *St Madoc* SM 866183

In the rib-vaulted porch is an effigy of a late 13th century knight with his head on a pillow. The nave walls and font may be of c1200. The chancel has been enlarged and is dated 1789 and 1878.

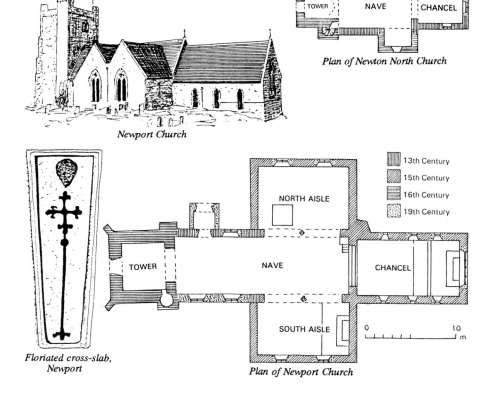

Plan of Newton North Church

Newport Church

13th Century
15th Century
16th Century
19th Century

NORTH AISLE

TOWER NAVE CHANCEL

SOUTH AISLE

*Floriated cross-slab,
Newport*

Plan of Newport Church

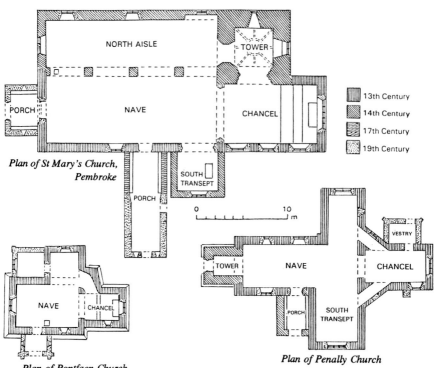

NORTH AISLE

TOWER

PORCH

NAVE

CHANCEL

13th Century
14th Century
17th Century
19th Century

*Plan of St Mary's Church,
Pembroke*

SOUTH
TRANSEPT

PORCH

0   10
          m

VESTRY

NAVE

CHANCEL

TOWER

NAVE

CHANCEL

PORCH

SOUTH
TRANSEPT

Plan of Pontfaen Church

Plan of Penally Church

St Mary's Church, Pembroke

PEMBROKE *St Mary* SR 984013

The oldest relics are a scalloped and cable-moulded font and the south doorway of c1200. Norman windows are said to have survived in the south wall until the 19th century. The chancel is late 13th century and the tower north of it and the north aisle with a four bay arcade on square piers are early 14th century. The west porch and south transept are of uncertain date. The inner part of the south porch has a vault and seats. The outer part is Victorian.

PEMBROKE *St Michael* SR 988014

The nave and equally wide south aisle are now mostly Victorian but the latter has a 13th century doorway near the east end, beyond which is now a tower in a very unusual position. The vaulted north chapel must also be at least partly medieval.

PENALLY *St Nicholas* SS 118992

The nave, chancel, and transepts with squints are all 13th century. The porch is 14th century and the tower is probably 16th century. Inside is a late 13th century altar tomb with an incised cross on the top with heads.

PONTFAEN *St Brynach* SN 022342

The church was a ruin in 1861. The small nave and chancel with a plain pointed arch between them are probably of c1200. The north transept and squint are later.

PRENDERGAST *St David* SM 956164

The NW tower is the chief remnant of the medieval church. The nave, chancel, north aisle, and north chapel are mostly 19th century work.

PWLLCROCHAN *St Mary* SR 921026

In a recess in the south wall is an effigy of Rector Ralph Beneger, d1342, with an inscription saying that he built the chancel and chapel. There are two other recess in the nave north wall which contains a 13th century doorway. The south transeptal tower with a plain corbelled parapet was built or remodelled when the north transept with a squint was added in the Tudor period. A north vestry was removed in the late 19th century. There are corbels for a rood beam in the nave.

REYNALTON *St Oswald* SN 090088

This tiny church has a south doorway, a south transept, and a vaulted west tower all probably 16th century although the main body walls are probably earlier and the font is Norman.

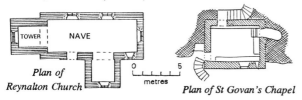

TOWER | NAVE

Plan of Reynalton Church

0   5
metres

Plan of St Govan's Chapel

Pwllcrochan Church

Rhoscrowther Church

St Govan's Chapel

REYNASTON *Dedication Unknown* SM 984257

This tiny 13th century chapel in Ambleston Parish was abandoned c1800 and is now a ruin in a farmyard. There seems to have been a room over the vaulted west porch.

RHOSCROWTHER *St Decuman* SM 903022

The nave north and south doorways look 13th century. The south transeptal tower has 17th century corner pinnacles but the lower part is earlier than the two bay south chapel with 14th century windows. Under the tower are two inscribed cross-slabs and a female effigy. The north transept or Hendleton Chapel contains the pedestal of a 15th century shrine and is the same size as the vaulted north porch bearing shields inscribed EL and Mary. The vestry lies on the site of the cell of St Decuman.

ROBESTON WATHERN *Dedication Unknown* SN 084156

The west tower is 13th century. The nave and chancel were mostly rebuilt in the 19th century, and the south transept and north aisle are also of that date.

ROBESTON WEST *St Andrew* SM 885096

A tower with features of c1500 but probably older masonry lies between the north chapel and porch. A female effigy lies under an arch of the chapel arcade and on the pier is a brass inscription with symbols of death to Thomas Cozens and four of his children who died in infancy. The font is Norman. The nave and chancel are probably 13th century. It is unlikely that the chapel formed the original nave as is claimed.

ROCH *St Mary* SM 882212

The font is probably of c1200. The 15th century south porch has a rib-vaulted ceiling. The rest has been rebuilt since 1800 when the chancel arch was raised and a 16th century south chapel demolished, its arches to the nave and chancel being blocked up. In the porch is a former churchyard cross-head depicting St Mary & St John, The Virgin & Child, a bishop and what is probably the Good Shepherd with a lamb.

ROSEMARKET *St Ismael* SM 953081

The nave and chancel are probably 13th century but have Victorian openings. The porch may be 14th century. The north transept has a squint and a round arch towards the nave. It has 16th century windows but is older. A Norman font has been re-cut.

ST BRIDES *St Bride* SM 803109

The nave, chancel, north transept and south porch are all 13th century. Only two of the lancets are unrestored. The porch outer entrance has just one long stone on each side. There are three grave-slabs, one showing a priest and another a floriated cross.

ST DANIELS *St Deiniol* SM 982004

The nave and chancel are of the same width and have pointed tunnel vaults. Both are 13th century although the nave is earlier. The tower and spire are probably 14th century. All the windows and doorways have been restored. The church is disused.

ST DOGWELLS *St Dogfael* SM 968279

The 16th century aisle has two arches towards each of the nave and chancel, which are both 13th century. The Strand family arms appear on the easternmost arch, the eastern part of the aisle being their chapel. There is a double bellcote.

ST FLORENCE *St Florencius* SN 082012

The nave, chancel, north transept, and south transeptal tower are all 13th century, and the porch is of c1300. East of the tower is a south chapel with a two bay arcade. On the north side of the chancel is a vaulted recess giving access to a vaulted vestry.

ST GOVANS *St Govan* SR 967929

This remarkable little barrel-vaulted chapel is squeezed into a cleft in the cliffs south of Bosherston. Doors in the west and north walls lead to steps down to the sea and up to the cliff-top respectively. Beside the altar is a doorway to a hole in the native rock.

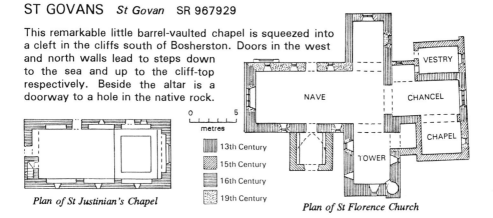

0   5
metres

▓ 13th Century
▓ 15th Century
▓ 16th Century
▓ 19th Century

Plan of St Justinian's Chapel

Plan of St Florence Church

St Non's Chapel

St Justinian's Chapel

ST ISHMAELS   *St Ishmael*   SM 831067

The 13th century nave and small chancel are connected by a narrow and sharply pointed arch. The north transept has a round arch towards the nave and a lancet in the squint to the chancel. The chancel has an original lancet and the nave has a blocked north doorway. The smaller south transept with a tomb recess and squint is Tudor. The porch may be medieval but has an 18th or 19th century outer arch of brick. The nave west wall is thickened to carry a double belfry.

ST ISSELLS   *St Issell*   SN 132058

Most of the church has been rebuilt but the four bay north arcade and the chancel arch are 14th century, the tower is 16th century, and there is a Late Norman font.

ST JUSTINIANS   *St Justinian*   SM 723252

This ruined building was built in the early 16th century by Bishop Vaughan. It has two doorways in the north wall, a staircase in the SW corner, and three bays of blind arcading on each side, with further arches in the end walls.

ST LAWRENCE   *St Lawrence*   SM 934276

The nave and chancel are 13th century. The chancel contains the rood-loft staircase. The vaulted porch and south doorway are 15th century.

St Petrox Church

*Piscina
Llangwm*

ST NICHOLAS   *St Nicholas*   SM 933396

The nave, chancel, and vaulted south transept with a squint are all probably 13th century but no old openings survive. A thick west wall carried a belfry.

ST NONS   *St Non*   SM 753443

Only the lower parts of this plain rectangular chapel now remain.

ST PATRICKS   *St Patrick*   SM 734272

Excavations in 1924 revealed foundations of an early single chamber about 11m long containing several skeletons. Little now remains visible.

ST PETROX   *St Pedrog*   SR 971976

The 13th century west tower, nave, north transept and south porch all have pointed tunnel-vaults. The chancel has been rebuilt. There is a brass to William Lloyd, d1674.

ST TWYNNELLS   *St Gwynnog*   SR 950976

The long 13th century nave has a pointed tunnel-vault carried on the thick side walls. Of the late 13th and 14th centuries are the small tower perched on the west wall, the south porch, the south transept with a squint and the arch of a former north transept. There is a plain tablet to Katherine Owen of Orielton, d1698. In 1259 a chapel-of-ease at Kylkermeran (Crickmarron Farm) is recorded. Nothing remains of it.

St Twynnells Church

Stackpole Elidor Church

SLEBECH   *St John*   SN 032138

In c1840 this church was unroofed and the 15th century effigies of Sir John Wogan and his wife were removed to a new church built in a more convenient location. They probably partly funded the building of the big new chancel, although until 1536 the church belonged to the Knights Hospitaller and it was only a parish church from the mid 17th century onwards. The nave is 13th or 14th century. The tower on the north side with its lowest stage serving as a porch is late 15th century. The north transept was added immediately afterwards and has a fine moulded arch. The south transept is a rather later structure partly of brick with round windows.

SPITTAL   *St Mary*   SM 976229

The narrow arch towards a demolished north transept looks Norman so the nave may be of that date. It contains a Norman font. The 13th century chancel has a recess in the south wall. The porch is also medieval.

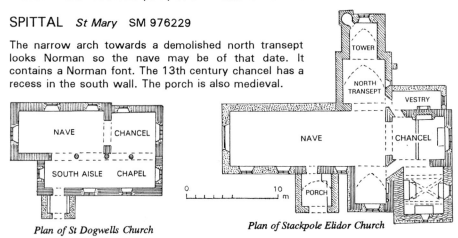

Plan of St Dogwells Church

Plan of Stackpole Elidor Church

STACKPOLE ELIDOR (CHERITON) *St James & St Elidyr* SR 988974

There are transepts of c1300 with pointed tunnel-vaults and squints and the slightly later tower lies in an unusual position beyond the north transept. The south porch has a tunnel vault and the south chapel a rib-vault. In the chapel is a monument to Roger Lort, d1613, an effigy of Margaret, wife of Richard Stackpole and two other 14th century female effigies. Richard's own cross-legged effigy with a dog at his feet lies under a fine canopied tomb recess in the chancel north wall.

STEYNTON *St Peter & St Cewydd* SM 918078

The west tower, north porch, and several chancel windows are 15th century. The plain chancel arch dates the nave to the early 13th century. Aisles with arcades of three bays with square piers were added in the 14th century. The font is Norman.

TALBENNY *St Mary* SM 844122

The nave windows and chancel are of 1893. The nave walls and plain pointed chancel arch are 13th century. The double bellcote on the thick west wall is 15th century.

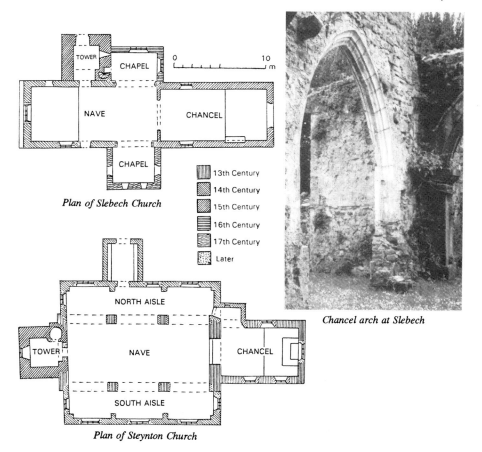

0   10 m

Plan of Slebech Church

13th Century
14th Century
15th Century
16th Century
17th Century
Later

Chancel arch at Slebech

Plan of Steynton Church

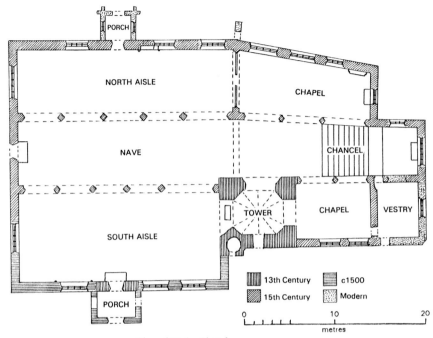

Plan of Tenby Church

TENBY *St Mary* SN 134004

This is the largest medieval parish church in Wales and a testimony to the prosperity of Tenby in the late medieval period. The south doorway and the lower parts of the tower are 13th century, and the SE vestry and north porch are Victorian. The rest is all of c1450-1510. A cruciform two storey west porch built in the 1490s was removed in 1831. The nave has very wide aisles with arcades of five bays. There must have been a south aisle by the 13th century but it was widened c1500 when the chancel arch was removed and coved wagon-roofs provided over the nave, chancel, and north chapel. The north aisle was added in the early 15th century but widened and heightened later. The long chancel is flanked on the north side by the irregularly-shaped St Nicholas' chapel of c1475-80 with a three bay arcade and an east window of 1885. On the south side lies the tower with a later spire rising to 45m, and St Thomas' chapel with a two bay arcade and a piscina probably reset from the chancel.

In the north aisle are a 14th century female effigy, a wall monument to John Moore, d1639, and a 15th century effigy of a skeleton representing John Denby, Archdeacon of St Davids. In the north chapel are the effigies of a 15th century merchant, Rector Hugo ap Owen, c1450, Margaret ap Rhys, d1610, and Robert Tully, Bishop of St Davids, d1482. The brass of the latter is modern. In the south chapel are monuments to Thomas White and his son John, both 15th century mayors, Ralph Mercer d1613, William Risam d1633, John Roch, d1670, Thomas Roch, d1693, and Isabella Verney, d1465, plus a 15th century font and bell lettered "Sancta Anna". The pulpit is dated 1634. In the churchyard is one wall of a two storey building thought to have been a chantry chapel with a dwelling room for the priest above it.

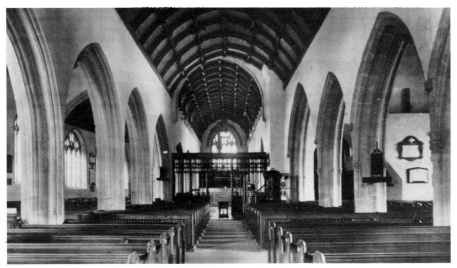

Interior of Tenby Church

West front of Tenby Church

UZMASTON   *St David (or St Ishmael)*   SM 969144

The church has an unusual plan. The chancel has a north wall in line with the three bay arcade between a wider nave and a north aisle with a squint. Tiny chapels open off the SW corner of the chancel and SE corner of the nave, and a small gabled tower stands north of the aisle. The whole south side was rebuilt in 1870. In the porch is a tiny figure of a civilian under a canopy. There is a scalloped Late Norman font.

WALTON WEST   *All Saints*   SM 865127

The short west tower with an impossibly low doorway to its staircase in a SW turret is 14th century. The font is of c1200. The nave and chancel were also of that period but have been rebuilt above the foundations. There is a tiny female effigy. In the Lady Chapel is a rounded 10th century stone bearing a cross.

WALWYN'S CASTLE   *St James*   SM 873112

The tower top has been rebuilt with continuous corbelled courses and the nave and chancel have been rebuilt on the old foundations.

WARREN   *St Mary*   SR 933975

The lofty west tower has lancet belfry windows. The nave, south porch, and south transept are vaulted. They are 13th century but the windows have been renewed. The chancel was rebuilt in 1855. The porch has corbels for the beams of an upper floor.

WHITCHURCH   *St David*   SM 799254

The nave, chancel, and north transept with a squint are all probably late 13th century but the windows have been renewed.

WISTON   *St Mary*   SN 023180

The nave is 13th century but has Victorian windows. The chancel arch and blocked south doorway are pointed but the north doorway is round headed. The long chancel with roughcast walls may be later. The west tower is 14th century. The vaulted north porch with a ogival outer arch and a basin on each side is early 16th century.

YERBESTON   *St Leonard*   SN 064090

The plain pointed chancel arch date the nave and chancel to the 13th century. The north doorway, south porch, and perhaps also the belfry corbelled out above the west gable, are 16th century.

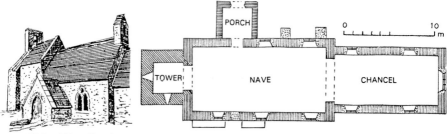

Walton West Church   *Plan of Wiston Church*

Haverfordwest: Brass

Chantry Chapel, Angle

Robeston West Church

MAP OF OLD CHURCHES IN PEMBROKESHIRE

The following churches are ancient foundations but have been rebuilt and lack old features: Cilgwyn, Clarbeston, Crinow, Ford, Little Newcastle, Llanfair-nant-Gwyn, Llanfair Nant-y-Gof, Llanfyrnach, Llangan, Llangolman, Maenchlochog, Manorowen, Meline, Monington, Morvil, Moylegrove, Nash, Penrydd, Puncheston, Redberth, St Dogmael's, Solva, Treffgarne, Walton East, Whitechurch.

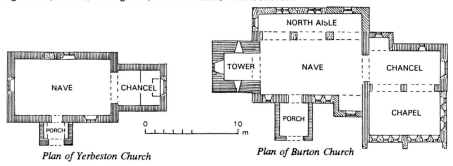

Plan of Yerbeston Church

Plan of Burton Church

INDEX OF WELSH CHURCHES

This is a master index of buildings described in all four of the volumes in this series which deal with Welsh churches up to c1760. Abbreviations are used as follows:

GG   - Vol 1 The Old Parish Churches of Gwent, Glamorgan & Gower 2nd edition (2003)
MW   - Vol 2 The Old Parish Churches of Mid-Wales 2nd edition (2003)
NW   - Vol 3 The Old Parish Churches of North Wales (1993)
SW   - Vol 4 The Old Parish Churches of South-West Wales (1994, 2003 reprint)
*   - Denotes picture on front or back cover